Literary America

LITERARY

A Chronicle of American Writers

from 1607-1952 with 173 Photographs of the

American Scene that Inspired Them

AMERICA

by David E. Scherman

and

Rosemarie Redlich

GREENWOOD PRESS, PUBLISHERS
WESTPORT, CONNECTICUT

Library of Congress Cataloging in Publication Data

Scherman, David Edward, 1916-
Literary America.

Reprint of the ed. published by Dodd, Mead, New York.
1. Literary landmarks--United States. I. Redlich, Rosemarie, joint author. II. Title.
PS141.S35 1978 810'.9 75-76
ISBN 0-8371-8017-1

Reprinted with the permission of Dodd, Mead & Company

Reprinted in 1978 by Greenwood Press, Inc.
51 Riverside Avenue, Westport, CT 06880

Printed in the United States of America

Excerpt from *The Age of Innocence* by Edith Wharton, copyright, 1920, D. Appleton & Company, reprinted by permission of the publishers, Appleton-Century-Crofts, Inc.; excerpt from *The First Gentleman of America* by James Branch Cabell, copyright, 1942, by James Branch Cabell, reprinted by permission of James Branch Cabell; excerpt from "One of the Missing" from *Collected Writings of Ambrose Bierce* with an introduction by Clifton Fadiman, copyright, 1946, by The Citadel Press, N. Y.; excerpt from *Life and Gabriella* by Ellen Glasgow, copyright, 1916, by Doubleday & Company, reprinted by permission of the author's Estate; excerpt from *Tobacco Road* by Erskine Caldwell, copyright, 1932, 1948, by Erskine Caldwell, reprinted by courtesy of Duell, Sloan & Pearce, Inc.; excerpt from "The Dry Salvages" from *Four Quartets*, copyright, 1943, by T. S. Eliot, reprinted by permission of Harcourt, Brace and Company, Inc., and Faber and Faber, Ltd.; excerpt from *Main Street* by Sinclair Lewis, copyright, 1920, by Harcourt, Brace and Company, Inc.; excerpt from *My Name Is Aram*, copyright, 1940, by William Saroyan, reprinted by permission of Harcourt, Brace and Company, Inc.; excerpt from *The Autobiography of Lincoln Steffens*, copyright, 1931, by Harcourt, Brace and Company, Inc.; excerpt from "Livvie" from *The Wide Net and Other Stories*, copyright, 1943, by Eudora Welty, reprinted by permission of Harcourt, Brace and Company, Inc.; excerpt from "Sonnet XXXVI" from *Fatal Interview*, published by Harper & Brothers, copyright, 1931, by Edna St. Vincent Millay; excerpt from "Renascence" from *Renascence and Other Poems*, published by Harper & Brothers, copyright, 1912, 1940, by Edna St. Vincent Millay; excerpt from "Good-bye and Keep Cold" from *New Hampshire* by Robert Frost, copyright, 1923, by Henry Holt and Company, Inc., copyright, 1951, by Robert Frost, used by permission of the publishers; excerpt from "Chicago" from *Chicago Poems* by Carl Sandburg, copyright, 1916, by Henry Holt and Company, Inc., copyright, 1944, by Carl Sandburg, used by permission of the publishers; excerpts from *Manhattan Transfer* by John Dos Passos, copyright, 1925, by John Dos Passos, published by Houghton Mifflin Company; excerpt from "Maggie, a Girl of the Streets" reprinted from *Twenty Stories* by Stephen Crane, by permission of Alfred A. Knopf, Inc.; excerpt from "Puzzled" reprinted from *One-Way Ticket* by Langston Hughes, by permission of Alfred A. Knopf, Inc., copyright, 1948, by Alfred A. Knopf, Inc.; excerpt from *Wickford Point* by John P. Marquand, copyright, 1939, by John P. Marquand, reprinted by courtesy of Little, Brown & Company; excerpt from Chapter XLVII, Book II, of *An American Tragedy* by Theodore Dreiser, copyright, 1925, by Horace Liveright, Inc., copyright, 1926, by Theodore Dreiser, used by special arrangement with Mrs. Theodore Dreiser; excerpt from "The Bridge" from *The Collected Poems of Hart Crane* by Hart Crane, published by Liveright Publishing Corporation, N. Y., copyright, Liveright, Inc., 1933; excerpt from *Coniston* by Winston Churchill, copyright, 1906, by The Macmillan Company, copyright, 1934, by Winston Churchill, reprinted by courtesy of the author's Estate; excerpt from *A Son of the Middle Border* by Hamlin Garland, copyright, 1923, by Hamlin Garland, and used with the permission of The Macmillan Company; excerpt from "Abraham Lincoln Walks at Midnight" from *Collected Poems of Vachel Lindsay*, copyright, 1925, by The Macmillan Company, and used with their permission; excerpt from *Gone With the Wind* by Margaret Mitchell, copyright, 1936, by Margaret Mitchell, and used with the permission of The Macmillan Company; excerpt from *Amaranth* by Edwin Arlington Robinson, copyright, 1934, by E. A. Robinson, and used with the permission of The Macmillan Company; excerpt from "Mr. Flood's Party" from *Collected Poems of Edwin Arlington Robinson*, copyright, 1937, by The Macmillan Company, and used with their permission; excerpt from *John Brown's Body*, published by Rinehart & Company, Inc., copyright, 1927, 1928, by Stephen Vincent Benét; excerpt from *Gas-house McGinty* by James T. Farrell, copyright, 1933, by Vanguard Press, Inc.; excerpts from "Percy Bysshe Shelley," "Washington McNeely," and "Isaiah Beethoven" from *Spoon River Anthology* by Edgar Lee Masters, copyright, 1915, by The Macmillan Company, copyright, 1942, by Edgar Lee Masters.

See page 176 for additional acknowledgments.

FOREWORD

In *Literary America* we have attempted, in pictures and words, to present the literature of this country, and the people who made it, from earliest days to the present. It is not a "picture history" in the usual sense of the phrase, since we have tried to avoid formal portraits of the authors themselves, their birthplaces, home-towns or their tombstones—in short, the photographic vital-statistics treatment of the popular history book. Instead, we have sought to convey pictorially the places which inspired their work or became famous because American authors wrote about them. We have in some cases resisted a literal documentation of these places in favor of a pictorial mood or impression that might illustrate better an author's own mood, or what we conceived that mood to be. This, we believe, brings a reader closer to the theme of American literature than a bare photographical recital of the accidents of birthplace or burial ground.

We were limited, to some extent, by the limitations of the medium: the decision to photograph real places and things in America (a task that took over two years and might have taken ten more) cut our original list of authors down to those who had stuck to their geography lessons. Many who wrote of an imaginary locale had to be excluded. Further, this consideration sometimes led to the exclusion of an author's most popular work and the inclusion of a lesser, but more photographable one. Finally, a significant site, located after painstaking research, would often refuse to lend itself to a suitable picture and had to be excluded.

In a land which has grown up as quickly as America, picturesque remnants of the past have not always been preserved with the best of care—though there are notable exceptions, such as those in New England and the California gold country. Similar literary pilgrimages which we made in England and France, for example, were perhaps more immediately fruitful. Nevertheless, this sometimes worked to our advantage: while the originally quaint avenue up which Ben Franklin strolled with his loaves of bread tucked beneath his arm exists no more, the present-day bustle of Market Street is possibly a more suitable commentary on Franklin's idea of civic growth than a tree-lined country lane in the heart of downtown Philadelphia.

Finally, the choice of material has been based on our own more or less fallible predilections. These were motivated by a desire to include, wherever possible, authors who had contributed significantly to the development of American literature in its different aspects as well as those who, while not really preeminent as writers, nevertheless remain very much a part of our living literature. This meant leaving out certain early writers who are now of more interest to scholars than to the reading public. As for twentieth century letters, we tried to confine the choice as best we could judge to modern classics. Only future generations of readers will select, out of the profusion of contemporary writing, what is to become truly living American literature.

ROSEMARIE REDLICH
DAVID E. SCHERMAN

TABLE OF CONTENTS

The front endpaper shows a rain-squall over the Mississippi River at Vicksburg. The back endpaper is a view of downtown Chicago from atop the Division Street gas-holder.

FOR JOHN

Jamestown church is oldest English colonial ruin.

. . . and arriuing at the place where wee are now seated, the Counsel was sworn, & the President elected, which for that yeare was Maister Edm. Maria Wingfield, where was made choice for our scituation, a verie fit place for the erecting of a great cittie, about which some contention passed betwixt Captaine Wingfield and Captaine Gosnold, notwithstanding all our prouision was brought a-shore, and with as much speede as might bee wee went about our fortification.

—A TRUE RELATION

CAPTAIN JOHN SMITH

The first book actually written in this country was *A True Relation of Such Occurrences and Accidents of Note As Hath Happened At Virginia*, and its author, Captain John Smith, became America's first historian when he found it necessary to defend his actions in the unhappy new colony against enemies in London. *A True Relation* is remembered today not only for its singular historical interest but for its simple, direct, and very personal style.

The Jamestown enterprise was pursued by trouble from its outset. The instructions of the Virginia Company to colonists aboard the "Sarah Constant," "Goodspeed," and "Discovery" were threefold: to find gold, to Christianize the Indians, and to establish another England in the New World. Gold was the major factor, and tales of gold so plentiful that the Indian natives tied up their prisoners in golden chains abounded in London. Of the 100-odd sick, bickering Englishmen who landed on the James River on May 14, 1607, only a few were accustomed to work. The rest—officials, impoverished gentlemen, traders, and servants—looked forward to an immediate life of wealth and leisure. It was Smith who saved the helpless colony from starvation by organizing the first barter expedition to the Indians. A seasoned adventurer, he took the realistic attitude that corn must be got by barter, ruse, or force, and thus set a pattern for future Anglo-American relations with the Indians.

In *A True Relation* Smith recounts his courteous reception at Werowocomoco by King Powhatan dressed in furs and pearls and surrounded by his women, but no mention is made of Pocahontas. Historians suspect that the incident of the king's favorite daughter's throwing herself on the body of the doomed soldier, which appears in his later *General Historie of Virginia*, was an invention of the doughty captain to capitalize on Pocahontas's later glamour in English society.

She lived and died in England after she became the wife of John Rolfe, a colonist who said when he married her he was doing it not for carnal desire but for the good of the colony and Christianity.

As for "James Citty," it never grew much beyond the original fort. Today, except for a few cellar holes, there is only a massive brick tower, probably that of the fourth church, to remind us of the first permanent English colony in America.

Local tradition says "Powhatan's Chimney" marks the site of Werowocomoco, Indian chief's capital.

Pocahontas, a tomboy in her youth, died an unhappy Stuart "lady" and is buried in England.

William Bradford

Thirteen years after Jamestown's establishment a very different kind of colonist landed farther north, at Cape Cod in what is now Massachusetts. These colonists were Separatists, Puritan radicals for whom even the reformed rule of English Presbyterianism didn't go far enough. Many who arrived on the "Mayflower" had fled earlier to Holland, whence they had planned their exodus to the new Israel. Among them was a young Yorkshire yeoman named William Bradford, who had spent the years in Holland studying Latin, Greek, Dutch, and the Bible. His judgment and integrity during the voyage had impressed his fellow Pilgrims, and when the first governor of Plymouth Plantation died, Bradford succeeded him and was re-elected thirty-one times.

Bradford wrote *Of Plimouth Plantation* as a conscious parallel to the biblical exodus. He felt it his duty to set down the long history of his people, dark and bright, their illnesses, disputes, and crimes, their steady ascent to prosperity, and above all their faith. His simple, direct style, permeated with Puritan spirituality and interlarded with Old Testament phrases, gives the book a heightened emotional appeal and a special charm. He wrote slowly, and stopped at 1646. The manuscript remained unpublished in his family, was stored in Old South Church tower in Boston during the Revolution, was lost, and turned up years later in the library of the Bishop of London, where it remained until 1896. A final and authoritative version was published only in 1912.

Bradford described the wintry Cape as a "hideous and desolate wilderness, full of wild beasts and men." When the colony moved on to more sheltered Plymouth, Provincetown became a kind of Coney Island for Indians and stray fishermen who, according to one old historian, carried on their "bacchanalian carousals . . . sometimes for weeks with unrestrained licence."

Famished Pilgrims under Miles Standish found and removed corn cached by the Indians among Cape Cod dunes near Truro. Spot is still called Corn Hill.

Provincetown today is a fishing town and resort.

. . . After longe beating at sea they fell with that land which is called Cape Cod. . . . And the next day they gott into the Cape-harbor wher they ridd in saftie. . . . Being thus arived in a good harbor and brought safe to land, they fell upon their knees and blessed the God of heaven, who had brought them over the vast and furious ocean, and delivered them from all the periles and miseries thereof, againe to set their feete on the firme and stable earth, their proper elemente.

—OF PLIMOUTH PLANTATION

Oct. 25, 1729: The Air clearing up this Morning, we were again agreeably surprized with a full Prospect of the Mountains. They discover'd themselves both to the North and South of us, on either side, not distant above ten Miles, according to our best Computation.

We cou'd now see those to the North rise in four distinct Ledges, one above another . . .

—HISTORY OF THE DIVIDING LINE

WILLIAM BYRD

By the beginning of the 1700's colonization of the coastal strip from Virginia to Massachusetts had progressed enough to present a definite contrast between the populated "tidewater" and the still uncharted hinterland called The Frontier, that famous locale which ever since has played such a creative role in shaping the character and institutions of America.

One of the liveliest accounts of The Frontier was left by Colonel William Byrd of Westover, a land-hungry Virginia aristocrat and man of letters whose *History of the Dividing Line*, diaries, and other writings earned him the title of "the American Pepys."

The event leading to the *History* was the survey of a 31-mile-wide strip of no-man's-land along the Virginia–North Carolina line which had been disputed for 47 years—an area to which, according to one horrified Virginia writer, "wicked and profligate persons retire, being out of the certain jurisdiction of either government."

A joint commission, including Byrd, got under way on March 5, 1728, at Currituck Inlet where a cedar post was erected as point of departure. The frontiersmen looked on the commission "as a troop of knights-errant running this great risk of our lives for the public weal," wrote the urbane Byrd, who noted that cattle and hogs roamed freely, that houses were built without metal, that a fresh hog-meat diet had resulted in widespread scurvy, and that most of the people dreaded being included in the stricter Virginia regime, choosing "rather to belong to Carolina where they pay no tribute to God or to Caesar."

Blue Ridge Mountains rise in misty tiers as William Byrd saw them at the end of the boundary survey in 1728.

Today's parish house in Danvers, Mass., stands not far from one where witchcraft delusion started.

And we have now with Horror seen the Discovery of such a Witchcraft! *An Army of* Devils *is horribly broke in upon the place which is the* Center, *and after a sort, the* First-born *of our* English *Settlements: and the Houses of the Good People there are fill'd with the doleful Shrieks of their Children and Servants, Tormented by Invisible Hands, with Tortures altogether preternatural.*

—WONDERS OF THE INVISIBLE WORLD

Cotton Mather

It was in the minister's house in tiny Salem village, now Danvers, that the terrible witchcraft delusion started which swept the Massachusetts Bay Colony in 1692. The story of how a number of "witches" around the town were blamed for the convulsive fits of some impressionable Puritan girls is a familiar one by now. Less familiar are the exact causes for the outburst of the delusion and its rapid spread. Bored, unmarried teen-agers were depressed by winter gloom and affected by a general anxiety that prevailed in the colony: increasing Indian raids and the loss of the Charter (meaning the end of the new Israel and the invalidation of land titles) plus a current belief that Doomsday was approaching, helped to set the stage for a popular hysteria.

Though Cotton Mather had no judicial connection with the trials at which the victims of the young girls were convicted, his writings on earlier "cases" and his oft-expounded views on the devil certainly did little toward allaying public fear and superstition among the faithful.

While others later repented publicly of their connection with the trials, Mather was delighted when asked to write the official version, published as *Wonders of the Invisible World.* The account was factual, but important omissions and its general tone allied him morally with the witch-hunters, and though later ridiculed, he still included in his famous *Magnalia Christi Americana* a large section on the workings of the devil in New England.

Mather's penchant for devils and occult doings is partially explained by his extraordinary personality. He was a prodigy who entered Harvard at eleven. Highly gifted, his talents were warped in the drab atmosphere of a dying theocracy. With a passion for knowledge, he developed an unhappy passion for praise and a dogmatic manner. The 470-odd publications bearing his name are a prodigious storehouse of fact and fable. His tragedy was to be born too late—the leadership of New England had passed from the Church to a rising merchant class.

"Gallows Hill" near Salem is still reluctantly identified by townsfolk.

Samuel Sewall

When Royal Governor Andros marched up State Street accompanied by none-too-eager Puritan dignitaries, Boston was 56 years old and still clustered around three hills: Copp's, Fort, and Beacon. The Town House toward which he walked was the seat of government of the new royal province and stood about where the venerable State House stands today. Less than a century later, "The Bloody Boston Massacre" took place almost under its windows and from its balcony the Declaration of Independence was first read to the people of Boston.

It is these years of transition from Puritan theocracy to royal province, with its accompanying resentment, that are reflected in Samuel Sewall's *Diary*. Nowhere else in the annals of New England do we get so detailed and vivid a record of public and private life as in these prosaic daily notes.

Starting as a young businessman under the tutelage of John Hull, his father-in-law, he soon became a deputy to the General Court, ran Boston's sole printing press, dealt in real estate, became a church leader, a special commissioner in the Salem witch trials, held several judgeships, and with the Bible as his only lawbook became finally the Chief Justice of Massachusetts.

Although his *Diary* is best remembered for the passages on his old-age courtship of Madam Winthrop, Sewall was first of all a family man who soberly attended and recorded the births, marriages, and deaths of his innumerable children, brothers, sisters-in-law, cousins, and friends. A devout Puritan, he had earlier approved harsh treatment for the Quakers and had supported the Salem trials (for which he later repented). He also inveighed against dancing masters, "naked breasts and arms and superstitious ribbons," and anything that might lead the young astray from traditions he believed it essential to uphold. Yet he was more kindly and urbane than most of his contemporaries, and in that sense looked rather toward the dawning eighteenth century than to his own dying society. Often remembered as "The Last Puritan," he represented perhaps more the first indigenous generation of the rising New England middle class, serious, devout, prudent, and prosperous.

Monday, Decr. 20, 1686. Governour Andros comes up in the Pinace, touches at the Castle, Lands at Govr. Leveret's wharf about 2 P.M. where the President, &c. meet him and so march up through the Guards of the 8 Companyes to the Town House, where part of the Commission read: He hath power to suspend Councillors and to appoint others if the number be reduced to less than Seven. He and Council to make Laws. Then took the Oath of Allegiance and as Governour, then about eight of the Council sworn. Court clear'd.

—SAMUEL SEWALL'S DIARY

Samuel Sewall lies with his huge family and his in-laws in Boston's Old Granary burial ground.

Wedged between office buildings, Boston State House stands as reminder of royal rule and revolt against it.

The "Great Awakening" flourished in Northampton.

The town of Northampton is of about eighty-two years standing, and has now about 200 families; which mostly dwell more compactly together than any town of such a bigness in these parts of the country; which probably has been an occasion that both our corruptions *and* reformations *have been, from time to time, the more* swiftly *propagated . . .*

—A FAITHFUL NARRATIVE

Jonathan Edwards

When studious, 24-year-old Jonathan Edwards came to Northampton in 1727 to assist his aged grandfather Solomon Stoddard in the ministry, he found a beautiful, prosperous place. Center of northwestern Massachusetts, the town boasted an air of ease and refinement and its church was the strongest and largest outside Boston. Yet it seemed to the young theologian that a certain laxness had crept into the congregation and (as he wrote in his *Faithful Narrative* in 1736), "licentiousness prevailed among the youth; frequently both sexes getting together in what they called frolics, where they would spend the greater part of the night."

But Edwards, who had by now taken over the ministry, noted that by 1733 there was a stirring of conscience among the young: several formerly gay young women had been converted and the spirit was spreading. In this wave of regeneration he saw Northampton the center of a world-wide movement and himself God's instrument in it.

His exhortations started the revivals that later spread all over New England, culminating in "The Great Awakening." People flocked to the churches to be kindled by the inner light and reborn. Edwards reached a climax with the Enfield revival, when he preached his dreadful "Sinners in the hands of an angry God" and the congregation writhed in such agony at his feet that he had to stop and ask for silence.

The immoderate effects of a religious wave in which 3-year-old children swooned in fear of hell soon became apparent, and the fervor lessened. In Northampton an epidemic of "profane reading" broke out, setting off a quarrel between minister and parish that led eventually to Edwards's dismissal.

Today remembered chiefly and rather unfairly as preacher of "hell-fire and brimstone," Edwards in his early days had been well on his way toward evolving a more humane idealistic philosophy, based on his intense religious mysticism, that would have made him an intellectual leader of his age and a lasting influence on American thought. But he chose to bolster a dying Calvinism against the onslaught of eighteenth-century enlightenment, with his absolutist doctrines of the sovereign, divine will and total depravity. In the end, however, enlightenment won and Edwards's theology was swept away with the rest of the Calvinist world. Few remember him today as one of the most creative intellects eighteenth-century America produced.

Bas-relief of Jonathan Edwards hangs today in same church which ejected him as minister in 1751.

On Enfield, Conn., green lies a stone commemorating Edwards's most famous hysteria-provoking sermon.

Benjamin Franklin

He gave me . . . three great puffy rolls. . . . I . . . having no room in my pockets, walk'd off with a roll under each arm, and eating the other. Thus I went up Market-street as far as Fourth-street, passing by the door of Mr. Read, of my future wife's father; . . . she, standing at the door, saw me, and thought I made . . . a most awkward, ridiculous appearance.

—AUTOBIOGRAPHY OF BENJAMIN FRANKLIN

The scene Ben Franklin describes in his *Autobiography,* written in his old age for the edification of his son, took place just after his arrival in Philadelphia at the age of seventeen. He had run away from Boston, made his way there on foot and by boat, and arrived on a Sunday morning, with only a few pennies, hungry, dirty, his pockets stuffed with extra shirts and stockings.

Philadelphia itself was only about forty years old, a town of 5,000. It had fine wharves along the Delaware and straight, unpaved, right-angle streets lined with small red-brick houses, often surrounded by gardens and trees. Little of this is left, but if you wander a block away from lower Market Street you may come across such a relic as Elfreth's Alley (where Franklin is said to have once lived), which still breathes an air of colonial simplicity.

As Franklin rose from a poor apprentice and spread his activities into many fields until he was Philadelphia's chief citizen, so did the city expand. By 1776 it had 40,000 people and in the English-speaking world was second in size only to London. Franklin had become clerk of the General Assembly, postmaster, had started the first lending library, got the streets paved, established a police force, a fire company, a hospital, and an academy, later the University of Pennsylvania. He had invented a stove, the lightning rod, bifocal glasses, and conducted his famous electrical experiments. He was a justice of the peace, alderman, burgess, representative to the General Assembly and commissioner to Congress, colonial agent to England, envoy to France, Sweden, and Prussia. Author of innumerable tracts, pamphlets, and manifestoes, of *Poor Richard's Almanac* and of the world-famous *Autobiography,* he developed a style that was simple and full of wit and that marked him as the first writer of modern American prose. He was also our first sociologist and economist and the first American to be a citizen of the world.

Franklin was an eighteenth-century humanist, and one of the few democrats at the Constitutional Convention. A champion of unrestricted manhood suffrage, annual parliaments, a single-chamber legislature, he believed at the close of his life that government was good to the extent that it remained close to the governed.

Franklin's Philadelphia looked more like quaint Elfreth's Alley, hidden away near the waterfront.

Market and Fourth, more rustic when Franklin first saw his wife, are now the heart of the wholesale district.

Hector St. John de Crèvecœur

Precious soil, I say to myself, by what singular custom of law is it that thou wast made to constitute the riches of the freeholder? What should we American farmers be without the distinct possession of that soil? It feeds, it clothes us, from it we draw even a great exuberancy, our best meat, our richest drink, the very honey of our bees comes from this privileged spot.

—LETTERS FROM AN AMERICAN FARMER

Unlike many other historical places in America that have completely disappeared since colonial days, the Orange County, N. Y., farm described in *Letters from an American Farmer* has hardly changed. The house is modern, but the "good bottom land" is there, and even one or two of the "gigantic pines, which neither art nor cultivation can ever replace," remain on the hill.

The author, a French nobleman who often called himself "Mr. St. John" (St. Johnsbury, Vt., was named for him), was a humanist, a disciple of Rousseau, and an early scientific farmer who delighted in his life as an American freeholder in the Hudson Valley. Suspected of loyalist leanings during the Revolution, he left his farm, returning later to New York as French consul. Here his knowledge of farming (as attested by correspondence with Jefferson and Washington) helped promote U. S. and French amity.

Meadows of Pine Hill Farm in Orange County, N. Y., still flourish as when Crèvecœur enjoyed them.

Laughing Gulls wheel above the Florida keys.

JOHN JAMES AUDUBON

When John James Audubon, another lover of nature and the American landscape, went to Florida in 1831 he had at last won recognition in this country and his monumental *Birds of America* was being published in England. In it he introduced a new style in nature painting: birds were drawn not as stuffed specimens, but in their natural habitat.

To give a livelier and more human touch to the ornithological descriptions accompanying his paintings, Audubon included 60 essays called *Delineations of American Scenery and Character*, throwing sidelights on pioneer life in the Ohio and Mississippi Valleys, on hunting adventures, and on the Indians of whom this charming Frenchman of mysterious origin had an understanding common to few of his contemporaries.

. . . the Gulls and Terns, ever cheerful, gambolled over the water, exulting in the prospect of abundance . . . those hovering over head, so astonished us that we could for a while scarcely believe our eyes. . . . The air was darkened by whistling wings. . . .

—DELINEATIONS OF AMERICAN SCENERY AND CHARACTER

Paine got his New Rochelle farm as a reward for his services to U. S., though townspeople refused him the right to vote.

Tom Paine

In 1776, when Tom Paine, an English-born corset maker turned journalist, decided to stay with a retreating American army and write a series of broadsides called *The Crisis*, he was heartily welcomed by Washington, who knew how much "Old Common Sense" (as he was called) had helped the movement toward independence. The war was at such a low point that Washington had written "the game is pretty near up." An immediate, if minor, effect of the rousing lines of the first *Crisis* on the demoralized troops was the surprise attack on the Hessians at Trenton.

The fifth *Crisis* paper, written at just as critical a time—when the defeated army lay at Valley Forge and intrigues against Washington were growing—called for unity in the face of dissension and widespread defeatism.

Discredited and vilified by the Federalists in his last years, Tom Paine kept the lifelong friendship of Jefferson, who maintained that his style could not be exceeded in "perspicuity of expression, happiness of elucidation, and simple, unassuming language." Spokesman of the American Revolution, Paine was, with Jefferson and Franklin, author of a truly indigenous philosophy of democracy for the common man.

. . . These are the times that try men's souls. The summer soldier and the sunshine patriot will in this crisis, shrink from the service of his country; but he that stands it NOW, *deserves the love and thanks of man and woman. Tyranny, like hell, is not easily conquered . . .*

—THE CRISIS

The bedraggled Continental Army under General Washington crossed the icy Delaware here, near Trenton, N. J., its morale bolstered by Tom Paine's first *Crisis* paper.

Soldiers' huts at Valley Forge were constructed of mud and logs. Cooking was done outdoors.

. . . If we had not at this time a man in the field, we could, nevertheless, raise an army in a few weeks. . . . Here, gentlemen, is the enemy. Here is the army. The interest, the happiness of all America, is centered in this half-ruined spot. Come and help us. Here are laurels, come and share them. Here are Tories, come and help us to expel them. Here are Whigs that will make you welcome, and enemies that dread your coming.

—THE CRISIS

Old cannon guard Ft. Washington at Valley Forge.

THOMAS JEFFERSON

After his retirement in 1810 from public life, ex-President Thomas Jefferson could look forward to seventeen years in which to enjoy Monticello, his Virginia home. One of the few burdens that followed him there was his extensive correspondence. Altogether his letters amount to 26,000, making him, as he once jokingly said, "truly a man of letters."

The versatile author of the Declaration of Independence had always managed to find time for non-governmental pursuits, particularly architecture, and the plans for Monticello date back to his college days. The choice of the site was a new idea—nobody had thought of building on a mountaintop in those days. Everything in the house came from his brain or his workshops: the lumber came from his woods, the bricks, nails, and hardware were made under his direction. Gadgets such as his adjustable bookcase and portable writing desk were products of his fertile imagination.

As architect of the new American republic he had sought a building style in keeping with its spirit and found it in the style of Rome. He extended his admiration for Roman political forms to Roman architecture, which to him had an eternal quality more suited to the New World republic than were the "provincial, misshapen piles" of colonial homes.

His success is visible not only in such mansions as Shadwell, Farmington, and Bremo, but in his culminating achievement, the University of Virginia, which combines his genius as statesman, political philosopher, and architect.

The University was a lifelong dream. William and Mary, the only college in Virginia, he thought "too Episcopal, too eccentric in its position, exposed to all bilious diseases and now abandoned." His plan was for "an university on a plan so broad and liberal and modern, as to be worth patronizing with the public support and to be a temptation to the youth of other states to come and drink of the cup of knowledge."

The plan for the University of Virginia, the drafting of the Declaration of Independence (he was only thirty-three at the time), and the writing of *The Virginia Ordinance of Religious Freedom* were the three things for which he wanted to be remembered, as the self-written epitaph on his grave at Monticello testifies.

Jefferson's serpentine wall at the University of Virginia, called an "astonishing piece of virtuosity," is one brick thick, provides a twice-warmed place for plants.

Trees Jefferson planted still surround Monticello.

. . . I am retired to Monticello, where, in the bosom of my family, and surrounded by my books, I enjoy a repose to which I have been long a stranger. My mornings are devoted to correspondence. From breakfast to dinner, I am in my shops, my garden, or on horseback among my farms; from dinner to dark I give to society and recreation with my neighbors and friends; and from candle light to early bed-time, I read. My health is perfect; and my strength considerably reinforced by the activity of the course I pursue; perhaps it is as great as usually falls to the lot of near sixty-seven years of age. I talk of ploughs and harrows, seeding and harvesting, with my neighbors, and of politics too, if they choose, with as little reserve as the rest of my fellow citizens, and feel, at length the blessing of being free to say and do what I please, without being responsible for it to any mortal.

—LETTER TO GENERAL KOSCIUSKO,
February 26, 1810

Brick and marble grave under moss-festooned South Carolina cedars marks the Battle of Eutaw Springs.

Philip Freneau

One of the bloodier battles of the last phase of the American Revolution took place near a cool spring amid cedars and gray oaks on the Santee River in South Carolina. It was twenty puncheons of rum, left behind by the British, that cost the Americans the initial victory. Preoccupied with the rum and other booty, they were surprised by the returning British and suffered heavy losses. Today most of the new Santee Reservoir covers the battlefield, and all that remains is a few graves and tablets on higher ground.

Philip Freneau was the poet-chronicler of the Revolution. Sir Walter Scott said that *Eutaw Springs* was "as fine a thing as there is of this kind in the language," and acted upon his convictions by stealing a line from the poem without acknowledgment. Freneau's capture at sea in 1780 kindled in him a fierce hatred for the British and redoubled his enthusiasm for independence and a republican government.

When the battle for independence was won and the battle for a constitution began, Freneau, a Huguenot descendant raised in New York and New Jersey, turned editor and became spokesman for what Hamilton called "people of no particular importance." But in Jefferson's opinion "His paper saved our constitution which was galloping fast into monarchy. . . ."

Freneau had started out as a lyric poet, and though war and revolution turned him to satire and journalism, it was as a poet of nature that he made his greatest contribution to American letters. He was the first to introduce indigenous American objects significantly into poetry. Instead of singing praise of the English meadow lark and the Sussex weald, as was the fashion, he wrote of the whippoorwill, the honeysuckle, the pumpkin, and the American forest. Far ahead of his contemporaries, he sought an independent poetry and culture. But contemporary America was not interested in poetry after the Revolution and ignored Philip Freneau, who had to seek a livelihood elsewhere and died, a forgotten man, in a snowstorm on the flats near his New Jersey home.

At Eutaw springs the valiant died:
Their limbs with dust are cover'd o'er—
Weep on, ye springs, your tearful tide;
How many heroes are no more!

If in this wreck of ruin, they
Can yet be thought to claim a tear,
O smite thy gentle breast, and say
The friends of freedom slumber here!

Thou, who shalt trace this bloody plain,
If goodness rules thy generous breast,
Sigh for the wasted rural reign;
Sigh for the shepherds, sunk to rest!

Stranger, their humble graves adorn;
You too may fall, and ask a tear:
'Tis not the beauty of the morn
That proves the evening shall be clear—

Led by thy conquering genius, Greene,
The Britons they compelled to fly;
None distant viewed the fatal plain,
None grieved, in such a cause to die—

Now rest in peace, our patriot band;
Though far from nature's limits thrown,
We trust they find a happier land,
A brighter sunshine of their own.

—TO THE MEMORY OF THE BRAVE AMERICANS

Boulder in mountain glen near Palenville, N. Y., marks spot where "Rip Van Winkle" slept.

On waking, he found himself on the green knoll whence he had first seen the old man of the glen. He rubbed his eyes—it was a bright, sunny morning. . . . "Surely," thought Rip, "I have not slept here all night. . . . Oh! that flagon! that wicked flagon! . . . what excuse shall I make to Dame Van Winkle?"

—RIP VAN WINKLE

. . . Not far from this village, perhaps about two miles, there is a little valley, or rather lap of land, among high hills, which is one of the quietest places in the whole world. A small brook glides through it, with just murmur enough to lull one to repose . . . this sequestered glen has long been known by the name of SLEEPY HOLLOW . . .

—THE LEGEND OF SLEEPY HOLLOW

WASHINGTON IRVING

From boyhood Washington Irving had a pronounced love of antiquities, nature, and rustic scenery. A native New Yorker, he roamed the pleasant country north of the city, found quiet old Dutch villages and mossy churches between the Westchester hills and the Hudson. Here he indulged his love for the past, and later wrote that he knew every spot "where a murder or robbery had been committed or a ghost seen."

Soon the entire Hudson Valley was his province and source of inspiration. One Katrina Van Alen of Kinderhook, with whom he reputedly fell in love, became the charming Katrina Van Tassel of *Sleepy Hollow*, Brom Bones was a local bully named Brom Van Alstyne, and the redoubtable Ichabod Crane was an itinerant schoolteacher named Jesse Merwin.

The "Kaatskill Mountains," across the river, had a bewitching effect on the boyish Irving. "Never," he wrote, "shall I forget the effect of my first view of them . . . part wild, woody and rugged, part softened away into the graces of cultivation." It was from just such graces that old Rip had escaped.

Irving's first satirical "Diedrich Knickerbocker's" *A History of New-York* had been a success, but it was with *The Sketch Book*, including *Rip Van Winkle* and *The Legend of Sleepy Hollow*, that he won international acclaim as America's first professional man of letters. *The Sketch Book* became the first American fiction classic, and its author was given an official welcome on his return from a long sojourn in Europe as a diplomatic official.

For an American author, Washington Irving was curiously detached from the contemporary scene, and his best writing is less representative of life in the New World than of European remnants that lay here. "A genial loiterer in the twilight of the old," he is fittingly buried in Sleepy Hollow Cemetery, near Tarrytown, N. Y.

Sleepy Hollow is still a quiet little valley spanned by Headless Horseman Bridge where "Ichabod" fled.

Just above "Natty Bumppo's" cave near Cooperstown, N. Y., "Chingachgook, Last of the Mohicans," died.

. . . they were presently within a few yards of the rock. . . . The incessant washing of the water for centuries had so rounded its summit, that it resembled a large bee-hive. . . . Hurry remarked, as they floated slowly past, that this rock was well known to all the Indians in that part of the country, and that they were in the practise of using it as a mark, to designate the place of meeting, when separated by their hunts and marches.

—THE DEERSLAYER

The Deerslayer's Council Rock rises from Lake Otsego.

JAMES FENIMORE COOPER

Thanks to Fenimore Cooper, American scenery—lakes, mountains, waterfalls, and above all the vast forest—was first adequately displayed in fiction. The creation of Natty Bumppo, the "Deerslayer" and the "Leather-Stocking" of his tales, gave to world literature its first American character.

This ideal man in the state of nature is said to derive from one or several old hunters named Shipman living in the vicinity of Cooperstown, N. Y., the author's parental home-town, whose leather footgear earned them their name.

Cooper's imaginative escape into the forests of an earlier day reflects his discontent with a contemporary America. A man of republican conviction but aristocratic tastes who despised his country's expansion and money-grubbing passion, he yearned for the polished tradition of an old federalist order he knew was dying. Constantly at odds with the press, sometimes justified in his criticisms, often just a crank, he was denounced by countrymen who once had hailed him as the first genuinely American novelist, and died a crabbed old man.

Reelfoot Lake in Tennessee was named for a legendary clubfooted Indian brave who hunted there.

DAVY CROCKETT

. . . about this time one of my old neighbours, who had settled down on the lake . . . came to my house and told me he wanted me to go down and kill some bears. . . . He said they were extremely fat, and very plenty. I know'd that when they were fat, they were easily taken. . . . But I asked a bear no favours, no way, further than civility. . . . So I went home with him, and then went on down towards the Mississippi, and commenced hunting.

—A NARRATIVE OF THE LIFE OF DAVID CROCKETT

Davy Crockett of Tennessee was a man who could stare a panther to death, put a ball through the moon, lift a steamboat on his back; he weighed two hundred pounds at the age of eight with his feet clean and his stomach empty, and his voice was so loud it couldn't be described, only drawn.

The legend web has grown so thick around this fabulous character that many are not sure he really lived. The real Crockett of the *Narrative* was born in eastern Tennessee, moved in easy stages westward with the frontier, was a hunter, Indian fighter, congressman during the rising "coonskin democracy" of Andrew Jackson's presidency, and died defending the Alamo in Texas.

His bear-hunting days near Reelfoot Lake in the "Shakes" country (named for the earthquake of 1811 that formed the lake) and his settling in western Tennessee in 1822 are described in his *Narrative*, a literary document of the Jacksonian democracy believed the only authentic Crockett work.

Augustus Longstreet

Another man with a sense of humor who wrote about frontier life, though himself no backwoods "character," was Judge Augustus B. Longstreet. His story of the "gander-pulling" at Hawk's Gully was one of the many written while he rode the judicial circuit, later collected in the American humor classic, *Georgia Scenes.*

By the 1830's a new literature was emerging, and half a dozen writers began to exploit the picaresque life of their own frontiers, finding a ready audience in the East. Longstreet had an ear for the oddities of Georgia society—for horse swaps, races, fights, socials, and gander-pullings (at which men laid bets on which could gallop fastest past a suspended grease-necked goose, grab it, and hang on to it). It was all part of the violent, optimistic, assertive new culture, where wit made up for lack of education—a culture that has ever since influenced American thinking and politics.

. . . he laid off his gander-pulling ground on the nearest suitable unappropriated spot . . . between Harrisburg and Hawk's Gully, to the south of the road. . . .

When "Satterday of thes pressents munth," *rolled round, I determined to go to the gander-pulling. . . .*

—GEORGIA SCENES

Row of houses in Augusta's Hawk's Gully marks site of Longstreet's "gander-pulling."

Legends say warriors erected this rocky cairn over the grave of an Indian girl near Stockbridge, Mass.

William Cullen Bryant

William Cullen Bryant never set out to be a poet. After he had left home in Cummington, Mass., to study law, his father found some poems tucked in a desk drawer—*Inscription for the Entrance to a Wood, Thanatopsis, To a Waterfowl,* and others upon which Bryant's fame rests. He took them to the *North American Review,* whose editors welcomed their new tone of gentle nature worship in the otherwise desertlike current literary scene.

Bryant's devotion to nature and the country life was fostered early by his physician-father, who taught the sickly boy the value of exercise by taking long walks and icy baths in nearby brooks. So well did he remember his lesson that even at eighty he preferred jumping over a wall to going through the gate.

Though he is remembered chiefly as a poet, Bryant became one of America's greatest newspaper editors. For fifty years under his guidance the New York *Evening Post* was one of the country's most influential papers, and Bryant himself turned from a Calvinistic Federalist into a Unitarian liberal, one of the early great crusaders against the Whigs and their burgeoning money philosophy.

. . . There was scooped,
Upon the mountain's southern slope, a grave;
And there they laid her, in the very garb
With which the maiden decked herself for death,
With the same withering wild-flowers in her hair.
And o'er the mould that covered her, the tribe
Built up simple monument, a cone
Of small loose stones. Thenceforward all who passed,
Hunter, and dame, and virgin, laid a stone
In silence on the pile. It stands there yet. . . .

—MONUMENT MOUNTAIN

Monument Mountain tells how a maid ended her unhappy tribal love affair by leaping from its crags.

The leaf-strewn entrance to Bryant's wood is near home of the author's father in Cummington, Mass.

Stranger, if thou hast learned a truth which needs
No school of long experience, that the world
Is full of guilt and misery, and hast seen
Enough of all its sorrows, crimes, and cares,
To tire thee of it, enter this wild wood
And view the haunts of Nature. . . .

—INSCRIPTION FOR THE ENTRANCE TO A WOOD

Whenever I looked out on the pond it impressed me like a tarn high up on the side of a mountain, its bottom far above the surface of other lakes, and, as the sun arose, I saw it throwing off its nightly clothing of mist, and here and there, by degrees, its soft ripples or its smooth reflecting surface was revealed, while the mists, like ghosts, were stealthily withdrawing in every direction into the woods, as at the breaking up of some nocturnal conventicle.

—WALDEN

HENRY DAVID THOREAU

In the spring of 1845 Henry David Thoreau went to Walden Pond, south of Concord, Massachusetts, cleared ground, and built himself a hut whose exact location was only recently rediscovered. He lived there for two years, long enough to write one of the few great and truly original books in American literature. Today both book and site are famous, though the latter is perhaps more visited than the former read.

Only a few of his old pines show their ragged stumps around Walden, and what was once Thoreau's beanfield can barely be traced. But it's still possible, of a sunny summer dawn, to sit near the unchanged pond, watch the mists rise, and listen to the songs of birds and buzz of insects that Thoreau knew.

Thoreau went to the woods because he "wished to live deliberately, to front only the essential facts of life," and not, when it came time to die, discover that he had not lived. It seemed to him, as he looked around tiny Concord and then around nineteenth-century America, that too many people were leading "lives of quiet desperation," that civilization had become overloaded with the "lower economies," that his countrymen were frittering away their lives with the details and not the essence of living. Men had become "tools of their tools," and mid-century industrialism had degraded not merely the poor who lived in shanties along the railroads of Europe and America, but the rich who lived in too-elaborate mansions. Thoreau sought greater freedom for the individual and more chance for him to develop creatively. Man could be happier

Dawn mists rise over Walden Pond in Concord.

and richer, and civilization a blessing, if he turned to nature and stripped off his useless burdens.

Thoreau wrote that he had "traveled a good deal" in Concord, but his knowledge of the rest of New England was as extensive as his Concord travels were intensive. His usual mode of travel was not by railroad, which he detested, but on foot, and in this manner he made four trips on Cape Cod "to get a better view of the ocean." The result was a book called *Cape Cod*. Unlike the more famous *Walden*, which was largely concerned with nature and ideas, *Cape Cod* talks of the country and its people. Some today find it his most charming and human book.

A simple stone marker in the family plot marks Thoreau's grave in Concord's Sleepy Hollow Cemetery.

"Fitchburg Railroad," now the Boston & Maine, still skirts the edge of Thoreau's Walden Pond.

We do not ride the railroad; it rides upon us. Did you ever think what those sleepers are that underlie the railroad? Each one is a man, an Irishman, or a Yankee man. The rails are laid on them, and they are covered with sand, and the cars run smoothly over them. They are sound sleepers, I assure you.

—WALDEN

Thoreau visited Highland Light on Cape Cod.

According to the light-house keeper, the Cape is wasting here on both sides, though most on the eastern. . . . One old inhabitant told us that when the light-house was built, in 1798, it was calculated that it would stand forty-five years, allowing the bank to waste one length of fence each year, "but," said he, "there it is.". . .

—CAPE COD

Edgar Allan Poe

Edgar Allan Poe's *Gold-Bug* is one of the few stories he wrote with an American background. The country he describes is that of the Charleston, S. C., area, with imaginative additions typical of Poe. It was a region he learned to know while stationed as a soldier at Fort Moultrie on the tip of nearby Sullivan's Island—a region full of pirate and Revolutionary lore. Never overburdened with military duty, he had time to roam the palm- and myrtle-covered sandhills stretching inland and watch the strange tidewater birds, butterflies, and beetles, all dominated by a rather melancholy seascape. He indulged in poetic license when he wrote of hills and cliffs, for the countryside is a dreary expanse of sand dunes and low woodlands, and the giant tulip tree of the *Gold-Bug* is nonexistent.

The mysterious bug itself, "*Scarabœus caput hominis,*" scholars agree is a composite of two species of beetles found on Sullivan's Island: *Caleichroma splendidum,* with a gleaming gold head and dull golden underside, and *Alaus oculatus,* the click beetle, whose two eyelike black spots on its prothorax give it a piratical, skull-like appearance.

Generally regarded as the "father" of the short story, the detective story, the horror story, and all of science fiction to follow, Poe had little immediate influence on contemporary writing in America. Looked at askance by a Victorian society which had little tolerance for his eccentricities, Poe found his first disciples among the European "decadents," particularly Baudelaire, de L'Isle Adam, and Mallarmé, who welcomed him "with terror and delight."

A latter-day America, accustomed to psychological, almost clinical, analyses of its writers, recognizes in Poe a deeply disturbed personality, in lifelong flight from himself, a poet whose genius lay in his ability to build a rational superstructure on his world of delusions and hallucinations and to create stories that twentieth-century readers could appreciate.

Poe's cottage in New York City's Fordham stood in open fields when he leased it in 1846 for his dying child-wife. It served as model for his tale *Landor's Cottage.*

Carolina oaks covered with Spanish moss like this one identified site where *Gold-Bug* treasure lay.

. . . Jupiter, by direction of his master, proceeded to clear for us a path to the foot of an enormously tall tulip-tree, which stood, with some eight or ten oaks, upon the level, and far surpassed them all. . . .

—THE GOLD-BUG

Woods around Concord were Emerson's "garden."

. . . In the woods, too, a man casts off his years, as the snake his slough, and at what period soever of life, is always a child. . . . In the woods, we return to reason and faith. . . . Standing on the bare ground,—my head bathed by the blithe air, and uplifted into infinite space,—all mean egotism vanishes. I become a transparent eye-ball; I am nothing; I see all; the currents of the Universal Being circulate through me; I am part or parcel of God. . . .

—NATURE

Ralph Waldo Emerson

In 1838 Ralph Waldo Emerson wrote in his journal that before he settled in Concord and roamed the surrounding woods his idea of nature had been a highly artificial one. Though nurtured on the English romantic poets and "bred in an oratorio of praises of nature," he found he knew the real thing only skin-deep. Once started on his trips to the woods, he found a new world. They became the study where he did his thinking; "all my thoughts are foresters . . ." he wrote. "I have scarcely a daydream on which the breath of the pines has not blown, and their shadows moved." The white pine was his favorite tree and he later bought a grove on Walden where he saw the pine as "nature's Aeolian Harp . . . an untamable Norse wood-God, hoary, ancient and wise in all things."

The aim of *Nature,* the first statement of his basic philosophy, was to find a scheme of unity between God, the soul, and nature. Written largely in the Old Manse in Concord, it sold only a few copies when published in 1836, but it became the bible of the small Boston coterie who called themselves "Transcendentalists" and won wider popular acclaim in England, where it was hailed by Thomas Carlyle.

Emerson benefited by Concord, but Concord surely didn't suffer from his settling down among its low hills and meadows. He was frequently asked to contribute to local historic celebrations, and on one occasion he wrote the dedication for the monument commemorating the Battle of Concord. As the *Concord Hymn,* its first stanza is a standard American schoolbook item.

A concrete "rude bridge" now spans Concord River.

By the rude bridge that arched the flood,
Their flag to April's breeze unfurled,
Here once the embattled farmers stood
And fired the shot heard round the world . . .

The foe long since in silence slept;
Alike the conqueror silent sleeps;
And Time the ruined bridge has swept
Down the dark stream which seaward creeps.

—CONCORD HYMN

A fierce eagle still guards the Salem Custom House.

. . . Over the entrance hovers an enormous specimen of the American eagle, with outspread wings, a shield before her breast, and, if I recollect aright, a bunch of intermingled thunderbolts and barbed arrows in each claw. With the customary infirmity of temper that characterizes this unhappy fowl, she appears, by the fierceness of her beak and eye, and the general truculency of her attitude, to threaten mischief to the inoffensive community; and especially to warn all citizens, careful of their safety, against intruding on the premises which she overshadows with her wings. Nevertheless, vixenly as she looks, many people are seeking, at this very moment, to shelter themselves under the wing of the federal eagle; imagining, I presume, that her bosom has all the softness and snugness of an eider-down pillow. But she has no great tenderness, even in her best of moods, and, sooner or later,—oftener soon than late,—is apt to fling off her nestlings, with a scratch of her claw, a dab of her beak, or a rankling wound from her barbed arrows.

—THE SCARLET LETTER

NATHANIEL HAWTHORNE

Nathaniel Hawthorne said the uproar created in Salem when *The Scarlet Letter* appeared was unparalleled since witch times and that he would consider himself lucky if he escaped from the town without being tarred and feathered. This did not happen but he was *persona non grata* there for half a century. The trouble was the first chapter on the Custom House, in which Hawthorne described with mild satire the languid atmosphere, the gluttonous inspector, and the senile sea captains. He had added the humorous chapter on purpose, as he felt the novel was much too somber and would otherwise never succeed.

At best, the author's feelings about his native place were ambivalent. He said he disliked it, and never painted it in flattering hues, yet he returned repeatedly, after long intervals, and wove it into several of his major works.

Son of an aristocratic but already impoverished Salem sea captain's family, Hawthorne knew his local history and folklore. It is said that he got the idea for Maule's curse in *The House of the Seven Gables* from a curse that Rebecca Nurse had put on his own ancestor John Hathorne, who condemned her to death as a witch. When a cousin of his bought the place, Nathaniel became well acquainted with the seven-gabled mansion and its secret passageway behind the huge chimney.

He left Salem when he married Sophia Peabody and settled in Rev. William Emerson's venerable house in Concord, which he named the Old Manse. Here they lived a classic marital idyll, the simple, secluded life, as he noted in their joint journal, but full of rustic pleasures: fishing, swimming, rowing an old boat of Thoreau's, hoeing the garden, reading Shakespeare or Milton to each other after tea. *Mosses from an Old Manse* resulted from this period.

Back again in Salem as customs surveyor, he wrote *The Scarlet Letter* and at last gained recognition as one of America's great new writers. He left town soon thereafter and never returned.

The twelve years before his marriage, which he lived as a studious recluse, creeping out of his mother's house only at dusk, furnished him with his major literary theme: that aloofness—separateness from society, lack of sympathy with fellow creatures—was the greatest sin of mankind.

Hawthorne named Concord home the Old Manse.

. . . How gently, too, did the sight of the Old Manse—best seen from the river, overshadowed with its willows, and all environed about with the foliage of its orchard and avenue—how gently did its gray, homely aspect rebuke the speculative extravagances of the day! . . .

—MOSSES FROM AN OLD MANSE

Nathaniel Hawthorne

The House of the Seven Gables was built in 1686.

Half-way down a by-street of one of our New England towns stands a rusty wooden house, with seven acutely peaked gables, facing towards various points of the compass. . . .

The aspect of the venerable mansion has always affected me like a human countenance, bearing the traces not merely of outward storm and sunshine, but expressive, also, of the long lapse of mortal life, and accompanying vicissitudes that have passed within.

—THE HOUSE OF THE SEVEN GABLES

Henry Wadsworth Longfellow

Henry Wadsworth Longfellow's name is probably connected with more American places than that of any other writer, with the possible exception of Whitman. As a Harvard professor and son of two prominent New England families, he had the conscious desire to create for America a national literary tradition that would embody his country's mythological origins as the sagas and ballads had done for Europe.

His *Song of Hiawatha* is the most famous of these long, narrative attempts to deal with America's native beginnings. Patterned after the Finnish Kalevala epic, it tells of the legendary Ojibway hero Manabozho, revered by Indian tribes from Lake Superior to Nova Scotia and the Rockies. The name Hiawatha he took from an Iroquois leader who lived around 1570 and was largely responsible for bringing peace and civilization to the newly formed Iroquois League.

Inspired by a daguerreotype of the "Laughing Water" falls near Minneapolis, he created the charming Minnehaha, daughter of the arrowmaker. The falls today are no mean factor in local Minneapolis tourist trade. They lie in a nicely landscaped park and are the Sunday goal of hundreds of picnickers. A thoughtful city government has added a number of pipes from the city water system so that friends of Minnehaha may not feel cheated during the dry summer months.

Longfellow often thought New England a rich source of material for the ballader. The Gloucester *Evening Journal* of Dec. 17, 1839, reported that "the Northern shore of our harbor presents a scene that makes the heart bleed—strewn as it is with wrecks and cargoes of 20 or 25 vessels, and here and there with the lifeless bleeding bodies of unfortunate mariners." Inspired by these catastrophes, most of which took place on a reef called Norman's Woe, Longfellow penned his tragic ballad, *The Wreck of the Hesperus.*

A star among the Cambridge literati, bookish, genteel, and divorced from current life, Longfellow combined in his poetry romantic, moralistic, and sentimental thoughts, expressed in simple, carefully metered lyrics that appealed vastly to contemporary Victorian tastes and made him the most popular and beloved poet of his day.

And fast through the midnight dark and drear,
Through the whistling sleet and snow,
Like a sheeted ghost the vessel swept
Tow'rds the reef of Norman's Woe.

—THE WRECK OF THE HESPERUS

The treacherous reef of Norman's Woe still rises threateningly in outer Gloucester, Mass., harbor.

Henry Wadsworth Longfellow

Minnehaha Falls are in outskirts of Minneapolis.

With him dwelt his dark-eyed daughter,
Wayward as the Minnehaha,
With her moods of shade and sunshine,
Eyes that smiled and frowned alternate,
Feet as rapid as the river,
Tresses flowing like the water,
And as musical a laughter:
And he named her from the river,
From the water-fall he named her,
Minnehaha, Laughing Water.

—THE SONG OF HIAWATHA

Harvard Yard is a symbol of U. S. college tradition.

JAMES RUSSELL LOWELL

When James Russell Lowell was asked to write a poem for exercises honoring Harvard dead in the Civil War, the muse refused to come until a day before the event, when "something gave me a jog and the whole thing came out"—523 lines.

In his earlier days he was an abolitionist radical and wrote the humorous *Biglow Papers*, dialect tales of a stanchly democratic New England farmer. Lowell soon retired among his books and came to typify the truly blue-blooded Bostonian, who as Harvard professor and editor of the *Atlantic* and the *North American Review*, sat in judgment on all things cultural. He was ideally suited to represent the best in Boston (and therefore American) refinement as minister to the Court of St. James's.

To-day our Reverend Mother welcomes back
Her wisest Scholars, those who understood
The deeper teaching of their mystic tome,
And offered their fresh lives to make it good:
No lore of Greece or Rome,
No science peddling with the names of things,
Or reading stars to find inglorious fates,
Can lift our life with wings
Far from Death's idle gulf that for the many
waits, . . .

—COMMEMORATION ODE

"Old Ironsides" rests at Charlestown Navy Yard.

OLIVER WENDELL HOLMES

Ay, tear her tattered ensign down!
Long has it waved on high,
And many an eye has danced to see
That banner in the sky; . . .

Nail to the mast her holy flag,
Set every threadbare sail,
And give her to the god of storms,
The lightning and the gale!

—OLD IRONSIDES

In the autumn of 1830 a Boston paper ran a small paragraph that the frigate "Constitution," hero of the U. S. Navy, lay unseaworthy in Charlestown Navy Yard and would soon be destroyed. A Harvard law student was stirred by the item, wrote on a scrap of paper the poem *Old Ironsides* and sent it to the press. Reprinted by all the newspapers, it kindled a flame of patriotic feeling, an astonished Navy Secretary rescinded the routine order, the ship was saved, and overnight Oliver Wendell Holmes became known all over the country.

Famed for his *Autocrat of the Breakfast Table*, he was Boston's first wit, writer of occasional verse, a rationalist with aristocratic antecedents, a Back Bay rebel when it came to Calvinism, and a much-sought-after physician before becoming a Harvard professor of anatomy and physiology.

At last, after wasting some two or three hours on the "short cut," we got out by following an Indian trail,—Black Hawk's! How fair the scene through which it led! How could they let themselves be conquered, with such a country to fight for.

—SUMMER ON THE LAKES

MARGARET FULLER

When Sarah Margaret Fuller, often called the "high priestess of Transcendentalism," decided a tour of the West was the next best thing to a longed-for trip to Europe, her chief interest was the Indian. She had carefully read Schoolcraft and Catlin and the Cooper novels, and the plight of the Indians reminded her of the Lowell, Mass., mill workers whose downtrodden condition had for some time concerned her. In Illinois she followed Chief Black Hawk's trail and noted in *Summer on the Lakes*—which Horace Greeley called "one of the clearest delineations ever given of the Great Lakes and the Prairies"—that the Indians always chose the most beautiful sites for their villages.

Margaret Fuller was undoubtedly one of the most brilliant women of her era, and as author of *Woman in the Nineteenth Century*, one of the first to seek equality for women on the intellectual as well as the social level. Scholar, critic, teacher, co-founder with Emerson of the Transcendentalist *Dial*, she was renowned for her conversation and mainly responsible for making Goethe and the Italian romantics known in America. A person of deep conflicts, she was not done justice either by her male friends—who "apologized" for eccentricities that would have gone unnoticed in the twentieth century—or by her writing, considered inferior to her conversation.

She had her trip to Europe, eventually, as writer for her friend Greeley's *Tribune*. In Italy she met Mazzini, whom she had long admired, and married one of his followers, Count Angelo Ossoli. On her return to America she was drowned with her husband and infant son Angelino in a shipwreck off Fire Island.

Gigantic "Black Hawk" statue stands guard over his ancestral Rock River Valley at Oregon, Illinois.

Harriet Beecher Stowe

Bas-relief of Harriet Beecher Stowe and Henry W. Beecher is in Litchfield, Conn.

From time to time in the course of history, books appear that express the aspirations of a large number of people at a particular period. One such book was Paine's *Common Sense;* another, Harriet Beecher Stowe's *Uncle Tom's Cabin,* which, though not a work of art, captured the imagination of millions and contributed to the solution of a major crisis in United States history.

When published as a book in 1852, it ran through three editions in ten days; 10,000 copies a week were sold, 300,000 the first year, both North and South. In England 1,500,000 pirated copies sold during one year, and the book eventually appeared in thirty-two translations throughout the world.

Deeply religious, Mrs. Stowe appealed to humanitarians everywhere who felt slavery was traffic in Christian souls. Wife and daughter of prominent abolitionists, she lived in Cincinnati, across the river from slave territory, and later made a trip to Louisiana for an authentic picture of deep South plantation life. She visited Chopin Plantation in the Cane River Valley, at that time owned by Robert McAlpin, a New England kinsman of hers said to be the prototype for Simon Legree. Not much remains of old Chopin since the railroad passed across the land, and at least one "Uncle Tom's Cabin" was taken up to the Chicago Exposition and then lost; but there are tales among the local people that Tom lies buried on a wooded ridge where traces of an old slave cemetery remain.

After *Uncle Tom,* Mrs. Stowe devoted most of her writing to New England, of whose society and psychology she was a lifelong student. In *Poganuc People* she wrote not only a fictionalized account of her own childhood in Litchfield, Connecticut, but also an intimate and authentic history of New England village life in the early nineteenth century.

Bantam River near Litchfield, which Mrs. Stowe called "Poganuc River," was a childhood haunt.

. . . Down under the shade of dark hemlocks the river had worn a deep pool where the translucent water lay dark and still.

—POGANUC PEOPLE

Old slave cabin on Melrose Plantation in Louisiana stands near where "Uncle Tom" worked and died.

Tom heard no more; for he was following Sambo to the quarters. The quarters was a little sort of street of rude shanties, in a row, in a part of the plantation, far off from the house. They had a forlorn, brutal, forsaken air.

Tom's heart sunk when he saw them. . . .

—UNCLE TOM'S CABIN

Old Melrose plantation house resembles the gloomy one where "Simon Legree," Tom's master, lived.

Whittier Homestead stands near Haverhill, Mass.

Shut in from all the world without,
We sat the clean-winged hearth about,
Content to let the north-wind roar
In baffled rage at pane and door,
While the red logs before us beat
The frost-line back with tropic heat; . . .

—SNOW-BOUND

John Greenleaf Whittier

A "Quaker Puritan" scion of Massachusetts farmers, John Greenleaf Whittier all his life was fascinated by his region's folklore. He wrote in his first collection of legends and poems that "New England is full of romance . . . the great forest which our grandfathers penetrated—the red men—their struggle and their disappearance—the powwow and the war dance—the savage inroad and the English sally—the tale of superstition and the scene of witchcraft—all these are rich material of poetry."

He himself did pioneer work in collecting the legends and early proved to be a natural ballader. *Snow-Bound*, his most widely successful and popular narrative poem, gives a vibrant picture of his Haverhill childhood on the farm built by a Whittier great-great-grandfather soon after he arrived in America in 1638. The farm stands today unchanged in all its main features except for the electricity and a three-lane highway rushing past its door a hundred yards away. A substantial oak structure, comfortable by early standards but symbolic of the hard and simple life of the early farmers, it was his home for the first twenty-nine years of his life. Later, when forest and frontier had moved far to the west, he remembered it as "surrounded by woods in all directions."

To the frail Whittier, farm life was too tough an existence. His early interest in books and legends led him toward journalism, with poetry as a pleasant side line. He became a Quaker firebrand and agitator, the politician among abolitionists, and a gadfly to New England congressmen during the original "Great Debate." His impassioned prose and poetry against slavery were often directed at a clergy whose acceptance of it he fought as a Quaker and a Christian.

Only after the Civil War, when emancipation had been at least nominally won, did the aging Whittier emerge as the genial, easygoing "folk-bard" remembered today. Until recently the prominence given this last phase of his literary life by academic circles has obscured his earlier contributions to American literature and political freedom and tolerance.

Unharmed of thee in Wenham Lake
The mottled perch shall be:
A blue-eyed witch sits on the bank
And weaves her net for thee.

She weaves her golden hair; she sings
Her spell-song low and faint;
The wickedest witch in Salem jail
Is to that girl a saint.

. . . .

Oh, fair the face of Wenham Lake
Upon the young girl's shone;
Her tender mouth, her dreaming eyes,
Her yellow hair outblown.

—THE WITCH OF WENHAM

Clouds are mirrored in Wenham Lake near Ipswich, Mass., in the heart of the early witchcraft country.

Abraham Lincoln

Some months after the bloody battle of Gettysburg, the federal government decided to establish a national cemetery on part of the battlefield. Thousands on both sides had been killed, twenty thousand had been wounded, and scores were still dying every day.

The dedication ceremonies were set for Nov. 19, 1863, and Edward Everett, foremost orator of the day, was asked to make the main address. President Abraham Lincoln was invited only as a matter of polite routine, and the interstate committee organizing the event was not overenthusiastic when he announced that he, too, would say a few words.

On the appointed day, Everett skillfully delivered a carefully prepared address lasting two hours. A hymn was sung and the President introduced. He was nervous as he pulled out his address and fumbled for his glasses. He spoke in a rather high, metallic voice, with his unmistakable Kentucky accent, but he could be clearly heard, and though he went slowly his speech lasted less than three minutes. It seemed no speech at all and people were disappointed. So was Lincoln, who felt it hadn't gone over. But Everett congratulated him and wished he could flatter himself to think that he had come as near the central idea of the occasion in two hours as Lincoln had in two minutes.

Next day most papers buried Lincoln's speech in local and international news—Napoleon III, a boxing match, and Beecher's return got the play. Some editors accused him of making a stump speech, and one called his remarks silly. Even the few who appreciated it showed surprise that Lincoln was capable of such fine literary expression. They reflected a prevailing tone of condescension on the part of the educated toward the ex-farmboy and politician —a view that seems strange today when many of Lincoln's speeches and writings have become classics of lucid English prose and a part of the American people's literary heritage.

Gettysburg monument bearing Lincoln's famous address was erected on the spot where he delivered it.

Huge Gutzon Borglum head of Lincoln stands before his tomb in Springfield, Ill.

Fourscore and seven years ago our fathers brought forth on this continent a new nation, conceived in liberty and dedicated to the proposition that all men are created equal. . . .

—THE GETTYSBURG ADDRESS

George Washington Cable

In the heart of New Orleans stands a large four-story brick building. . . . With its gray stucco peeling off in broad patches, it has a solemn look of gentility in rags, and stands, or, as it were, hangs, about the corner of two ancient streets, like a faded fop who pretends to be looking for employment. . . .

—'SIEUR GEORGE

A new movement, the "local color" school, arose in the late nineteenth century. Tired of Gothic castles and far-off adventures, readers sought American locales, such as California, the colorful European settlements in the Midwest, or New Orleans.

Outstanding here were the stories of George Washington Cable, whose *Old Creole Days* first told the rest of the United States about that Baghdad, New Orleans of the Spanish-French era. As clerk in a cotton office, the Confederate soldier (who died in Northampton, Massachusetts, a champion of the Negro cause) pored over ancient documents and wrote intimate stories of French Quarter people and legends that even today are a delightful and useful introduction to the landmarks and atmosphere of the old town.

The 'Sieur George House stands in the old French Quarter of New Orleans.

Silver-green Marshes of Glynn stretch unendingly along the Georgia coast.

Sidney Lanier

When he lived in Brunswick, Ga., Sidney Lanier went daily, a flute hung over his shoulder, to his favorite spot near an inlet on the mainland. There under a moss-hung oak he would contemplate, at sunrise, noon, or sunset, the great marshes as they stretched toward the semitropical Sea Islands of St. Simon and Jekyll. He wrote, too, but was never satisfied with his lines until he had later settled in Baltimore, when *The Marshes of Glynn* took its final shape.

Lanier called his work "a symphony of bold design," for what he had attempted here and in the four other poems on which his fame rests was poetical harmony instead of simple melody. A virtuoso on the flute, he brought his devotion to music to his writing and wrote a book on the science of verse in which he tried to establish a parallel between music and poetry.

Oh, what is abroad in the marsh and the terminal
sea?
Somehow my soul seems suddenly free
From the weighing of fate and the sad discussion
of sin,
By the length and the breadth and the sweep of the
marshes of Glynn.

—THE MARSHES OF GLYNN

Lanier was a native Georgian whose great musical talent impressed neither his family nor a none too intellectually inclined plantation society. In spite of it all he was the leading poetic voice of the post-bellum South, a "poet of magnificent fragments."

Though many have fallen, some of Walt Whitman's redwoods still stand in California national forests.

Montauk lies at the easternmost tip of "fish-shaped Paumanok" (Long Island) where the poet was born.

. . . Along the northern coast,
Just back from the rock-bound shore and the caves,
In the saline air from the sea in the Mendocino country,
With the surge for base and accompaniment low and hoarse,
With crackling blows of axes sounding musically driven by strong arms,
Riven deep by the sharp tongues of the axes, there in the redwood forest dense,
I heard the mighty tree its death-chant chanting;
The choppers heard not, the camp shanties echoed not,
The quick-ear'd teamsters and chain and jack-screw men heard not,
As the wood-spirits came from their haunts of a thousand years to join the refrain,
But in my soul I plainly heard.

—SONG OF THE REDWOOD TREE

WALT WHITMAN

More than any other American poet, Walt Whitman tried to embody in his work the whole of America—from "blue Ontario's shores" to the Louisiana bayous, from the East's sea-swept coasts and the fertile valleys of the Midwest to the gigantic redwood forests of California which to him meant the vastness and strength of the country.

Born in Huntington, Long Island, of old English-Dutch stock, he loved the beaches and fields of his "Paumanok" and the sea whose vast blue expanse was his mystic "savage old mother."

"My infancy, childhood, youth, manhood," he wrote in *Specimen Days*, "were all pass'd on Long Island, which I sometimes feel as if I had incorporated. I roam'd, as a boy and man, and have lived in nearly all parts, from Brooklyn to Montauk Point." At the latter he "spent many hours on Turtle Hill by the old lighthouse, on the extreme point, looking out on the ceaseless roll of the Atlantic."

While trying to make a living as a hack journalist, printer, and odd-jobman in the city, he experimented with new poetic forms. The result was *Leaves of Grass*, a slim volume of twelve poems at first, run off by an obscure printer in Brooklyn. It was to be an American Bible, the beginning of a new national literature; and the first reception it got was devastating. It was "an impertinence towards the English language . . . an affront upon the recognized morality," "a mass of bombast, egotism, vulgarity and nonsense." Whittier threw his copy into the fireplace, and Lowell felt "this kind of thing won't do." Unexpectedly, Emerson found it "the most extraordinary piece of wit and wisdom that America has yet contributed." On the whole, America of the genteel Victorian age ignored him.

Transcendental mystic and disciple of Enlightenment, Walt Whitman was the first poet to reject wholeheartedly the Puritan ethical heritage. Influenced by the beginnings of evolutionary science and a revolutionary trend in religion, literature, and politics that swept the Western world in the forties and fifties, he proclaimed a new heaven on earth for America.

As he grew older and the Gilded Age got into full swing, Whitman saw most of his bold hopes fading. Unheeded by a country growing far too busily to stop for him, his influence made itself felt only on succeeding generations of poets and novelists here and abroad. His verses, written out of deep and lonely despair by a man who craved communion with others, are today still an inspiration to readers seeking a truer and better life.

Walt Whitman

Whitman liked to loiter along the ocean beaches of his native Long Island and watch the sea ebb.

Chaff, straw, splinters of wood, weeds, and the sea-gluten,
Scum, scales from shining rocks, leaves of salt-lettuce, left by the tide,
Miles walking, the sound of breaking waves the other side of me,
Paumanok there and then as I thought the old thought of likenesses, . . .

—AS I EBB'D WITH THE OCEAN OF LIFE

On Blennerhassett Island in the Ohio River, Aaron Burr once hatched the plot for his great conspiracy.

Bride of the swart Ohio;
Nude, yet fair to look upon,
Clothed only with the leaf,
As was innocent Eve of Eden.
The son of grim old Alleghany,
And white-breasted Monongahela
Is wedded to thee, and it is well. . . .

—ISLE OF LA BELLE RIVIÈRE

Emily saw the Amherst dawn from her windows.

I'll tell you how the sun rose,—
A ribbon at a time.
The steeples swam in amethyst,
The news like squirrels ran.

The hills untied their bonnets,
The bobolinks begun.
Then I said softly to myself,
"That must have been the sun!"

EMILY DICKINSON

While America was embarked on the greatest era of national expansion and exploitation the world had ever seen, one of her leading poets lived and died unnoticed, a recluse in a quiet New England college town. Decades later, Americans have come to realize that Emily Dickinson represented the last flowering of nineteenth-century New England culture and to recognize her as one of the country's foremost modern poets.

For this belated recognition a New England strict tradition, a dominant father, and her own personal ill fortune are all to blame. Edward Dickinson, a highly respected man who ruled his family with benevolent austerity, believed the Bible and the classics to be the only fit reading for his two spinster daughters. Though much of Emily's life is shrouded in mystery, it is believed that after a "normal" childhood, during which she showed a spirited imagination and a thirst for knowledge, she fell in love with someone she met, but could not marry, on one of her few trips outside her native Amherst. It brought the crisis of her life to this highly sensitive creature, and a careful study of her poems and letters shows that after a period of apparent nervous collapse she saved herself by turning to poetry. She had been writing since girlhood, but she did not emerge as an artist until she was able to accept and sublimate this most crucial disappointment. "Only when she realized that the deathblow to her heart had become the life-blow to her mind," wrote George F. Whicher, her most astute biographer, "was she able to view her grief objectively." To her Puritan sensibility eternity became her only escape and the grave appeared as a shining door to future reunion.

In nature she found her strongest support. By studying it intensively in the restricted area of her home she gained a universal understanding, and in its small, concrete facts she found fragments of reality to keep her in touch with the world.

Emily's garden in particular was a universe from which she drew quantities of her material. She had a "green thumb" and could make the frailest flowers thrive. For years neighbors saw "Miss Emily" among her flowers or playing with the children. Then, gradually, her neurotic shyness increased with ill-health and she withdrew completely within the parental home. Few people knew she was writing thousands of poems, and only after her death were they published and her position in American and world literature assured.

From window near desk where she did much of her writing, Emily looked out on her beloved garden.

New feet within my garden go,
New fingers stir the sod;
A troubadour upon the elm
Betrays the solitude.

Emily Dickinson

I died for beauty, but was scarce
Adjusted in the tomb,
When one who died for truth was lain
In an adjoining room.

He questioned softly why I failed?
"For beauty," I replied.
"And I for truth,—the two are one;
We brethren are," he said.

Emily's grave was only her gateway to eternity.

In the same New Bedford there stands a Whaleman's Chapel, and few are the moody fishermen, shortly bound for the Indian Ocean or Pacific, who fail to make a Sunday visit to the spot. . . . Entering, I found a small scattered congregation of sailors and sailors' wives and widows . . . and there these silent islands of men and women sat steadfastly eyeing several marble tablets, with black borders, . . . Three of them ran something like the following, but I do not pretend to quote:—

—MOBY DICK

HERMAN MELVILLE

Herman Melville wrote the chapters about New Bedford in *Moby Dick* from firsthand experience. Like Ishmael, his lonely wanderer who came to the greatest whaling port in New England to join the crew of the "Pequod," Melville had come there in the winter of 1841, at the age of twenty-two, to join the "Acushnet," leaving from Fairhaven for the South Pacific.

Here he doubtless came to know the dark taverns along the waterfront where Ishmael had his first forebodings of the fateful trip and met Queequeg, the harpooner. The taverns have given way to warehouses and antique shops, but another landmark, unforgettably described by Melville, the Seamen's Bethel, still stands.

A gray wooden structure opposite the Bourne Whaling Museum, it is still a place of worship for old mariners and their families. The famous crow's-nest pulpit where "Father Mapple" preached his memorable sermon was probably a victim of a fire that gutted the place in 1866, but the black-bordered marble tablets remain, and among the pews a place is even pointed out where Ishmael found the heathen Queequeg in apparent devotion.

Before he wrote *Moby Dick*, Melville studied all available whaling lore, but the story that seemed mainly to impress him was that of the "Essex," a Nantucket whaler actually stove in and sunk by a huge sperm whale in the Pacific in 1820. He had the story at first hand from Owen Chase, the "Essex's" first mate.

For a long time dismissed as "just a whaling yarn," *Moby Dick* has lately been recognized as one of the most complex and profound books ever written in America. A recent biographer, Newton Ar-

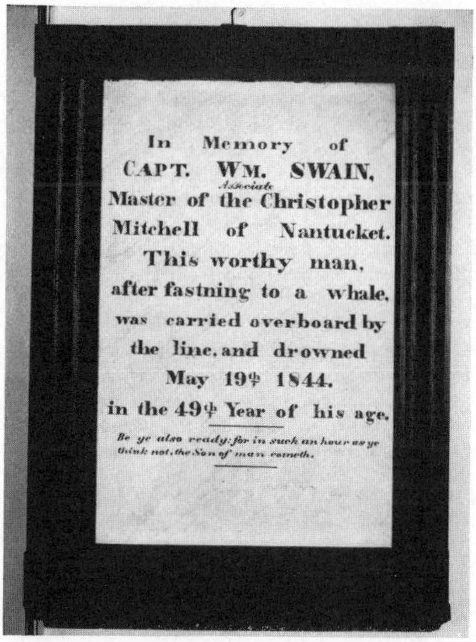

Beneath the black-bordered marble memorials in the Seamen's Bethel on Johnny Cake Hill, New Bedford, Ishmael heard Father Mapple preach, in *Moby Dick*.

vin, has shown it to be really four books: the story of a whaling voyage; the dreamlike projection of Melville's personal unconscious drives; a consideration of the moral climate of nineteenth-century America wherein Melville pondered the dilemma of Ahab, the modern "free" American whose individualism is at once sublime, heroic self-reliance and wild, anarchic egotism; and finally its meaning as a nature myth revealing Melville's nineteenth-century preoccupation with gigantic impersonal forces.

More than any other writer of his age Herman Melville, after service as a forecastle hand in the South Seas and years of mental isolation in Pittsfield and New York, penetrated the surface of what he called "snivelization," and what he found left him the blackest pessimist. When instead of tales of luscious South Sea life he offered his public such books as *Moby Dick* and *Pierre*, it turned from him in bewilderment and dislike and left him, the most tragic of the then current literary figures, to live and die ignored.

Melville chose Nantucket, which he didn't know, as the starting point for the "Pequod's" cruise, for no other port symbolized so clearly the genius of American whaling. Here the first whale was sighted in 1672, here the God-fearing Quaker whaling captains won renown for skill and daring comparable to that of the Elizabethan sea dogs.

Nantucket! Take out your map and look at it. See what a real corner of the world it occupies; how it stands there, away off shore, more lonely than the Eddystone lighthouse. Look at it—a mere hillock, and elbow of sand; all beach, without a background. There is more sand there than you would use in twenty years as a substitute for blotting paper.

—MOBY DICK

Brant Point Light guides sailors into Nantucket

Mount Whitney in the High Sierras raises its snowy head above the sandy California desert.

JOAQUIN MILLER

Afar the bright sierras lie
A swaying line of snowy white,
A fringe of heaven hung in sight
Against the blue base of the sky. . . .

—SONGS OF THE SIERRAS

Cincinnatus Hiner Miller was a Westerner the way Easterners liked them. Born in Indiana, he moved to Oregon, and later ran away to the gold camps, lived with Indians and begot a daughter named Cali-Shasta, taught school, practiced law, supported the Confederacy, was an editor and judge, fought Indians, married and deserted a second wife, wrote poetry in the hills, and descended upon San Francisco to be lionized by the local literati.

Thence he sailed to England, clad in jack boots, sombrero, and flashy bandanna, to which he later added a fur coat with gold-nugget buttons ("it helps sell the poems, boys, and tickles the duchesses!"). The English loved *Songs of the Sierras* for its sonorous verse and brilliant pictures. The aging bohemian later settled in the Oakland hills to practice and preach the simple life and advocate free love.

Mark Twain

Mark Twain hit Virginia City when it was still mining camp and "big town" rolled into one. It had grown, from its early days of "frame shanties, pitched together as if by accident" on the slope of Mount Davidson, to the star city of the Comstock Lode, with forty-two sumptuous saloons glittering with crystal chandeliers, bawdy sculptures, and marble bars, dance halls, theaters, three stock exchanges, four newspapers, and four churches. It was the only town in the West where the miners didn't have to travel from their digs to the pleasures and

The "city" of Virginia roosted royally midway up the steep side of Mount Davidson, seven thousand two hundred feet above the level of the sea, and in the clear Nevada atmosphere was visible from a distance of fifty miles!

—ROUGHING IT

Virginia City, Nev., pride of the Washoe and site of the Comstock Lode, is now a crumbling ghost town.

comforts of city life.

When Sam Clemens joined the staff of the *Territorial Enterprise* in 1862, after an unrewarding try at prospecting, it was the leading paper, rough and flamboyant but an honest and strong influence. He soon drew attention to himself with a series of journalistic hoaxes that went the rounds of all the camps, and in two years, under his pen name of Mark Twain, was the leading reporter of the West. *Roughing It* was his later account of the glorious pioneer-mining days, and it was snapped up by a public which bought 40,000 copies in the first three months.

Tom Sawyer appeared in 1876 and broke a long-standing taboo: its hero was neither a model of youthful manners nor a warning example of bad boy, but a normal kid with all his "natural cussedness." Both *Tom* and *Huck Finn*, his second boy masterpiece, were born of his memories of Hannibal, Mo., "that indolent semi-Southern town which slept for the most part like a cat in the sun, but stretched and rubbed its eyes when the Mississippi

I run the canoe into a deep dent in the bank that I knowed about; I had to part the willow branches to get in; and when I made fast nobody could 'a' seen the canoe from the outside.

—HUCKLEBERRY FINN

In a Mississippi River backwater opposite Hannibal hides an old flatboat like the one Huck Finn "borrowed."

A modern Mississippi steamboat lights up the river as it did when Huck floated by with Jim on their raft.

steamboats called." Here young Sam and his friends, John Briggs, Will Bowen, and the disreputable Tom Blankenship (the model for "Huck"), ran wild from Holiday's Hill ("Cardiff" in the book) to the caves south of town, into the woods and onto the Mississippi islands.

Huck and Tom were Mark Twain's defense of all American boys against the village mentality and the Sunday-school morality he knew so well from his own youth. He was trying to recapture some of these golden years at a time when he was beginning to show increasing literary concern about humanity's future in the era of America's Gilded Age.

Hailed as the "Lincoln of our literature" by William Dean Howells, Mark Twain seemed to fulfill Whitman's call for a real American writer. With no quasi-European or sectional viewpoint, but with deep roots in the country and a strong flavor of indigenous Western humor, he became our first great national literary figure.

The fifth night we passed St. Louis, and it was like the whole world lit up. In St. Petersburg they used to say there was twenty or thirty thousand people in St. Louis, but I never believed it till I see that wonderful spread of lights at two o'clock that still night. There warn't a sound there; everybody was asleep.

—HUCKLEBERRY FINN

This was once a busy street in Virginia City.

. . . Virginia had grown to be the "livest" town, for its age and population, that America had ever produced. The sidewalks swarmed with people—to such an extent, indeed, that it was generally no easy matter to stem the human tide. . . . So great was the pack, that buggies frequently had to wait half an hour for an opportunity to cross the principal street.

—ROUGHING IT

Bret Harte

When the oracular *Atlantic Monthly* reprinted *The Luck of Roaring Camp* by Francis Bret Harte, it created a literary sensation in the east second only to the one created by *Uncle Tom's Cabin* a decade earlier. Literature during the sixties was in a slump; magazines published mostly English authors, and editors yearned for American fiction. Harte's tale of a California mining camp answered the cry of readers for something about their own continent, and he reached national fame overnight.

Bret Harte was no novice at writing. He had a local reputation among budding literary groups in San Francisco, where he had worked for various magazines as editor and critic. His own ambition had been to become the "Irving of the California mission country" and to excel in "sophisticated" writing and poetry. The rough life of the gold camps was to him a subject fit only for satire and contempt, and he disagreed with those who saw rich literary gold in it. He succeeded in spite of himself.

Harte, the son of an educated and genteel but impoverished New York family, had come west as a young man, and he could never get over the feeling that he was an Eastern outcast lost in a wild, barbarous country. During his two years in the California gold country he did odd jobs as teacher, typesetter, clerk, and express messenger, and lived with a friend's mining gang near Melones on the Stanislaus River. In these green foothills, from Angel's Camp to Table Mountain, the quiet ghost towns and man-made mounds and caves along the rivers still bear witness to the gold frenzy that seized the new country a century ago.

After the success of *The Luck*, other mining-country stories by Harte were snapped up by Eastern papers and a collection appeared in book form. The *Atlantic* offered him the unheard-of sum of $10,000 a year for his stories, and Harte now knew where his fortune lay. He wrote *The Outcasts of Poker Flat*, *Tennessee's Partner*, and "The Heathen Chinee," and climaxed his career with a triumphal trip back east, where he was feted by the literary greats of the day. After seven years of writing in New York, during which he never developed beyond his original stories, he went to Germany and Scotland as U. S. consul, settled finally in England, and died there without ever returning to, or regretting, the West to which he owed his fame.

Harte was eager to husband his literary bonanza

I then turned toward the Wingdam Temperance Hotel. . . . It might have been called the "Total Abstinence" Hotel, from the lack of anything to intoxicate or inthrall the senses. It was designed with an eye to artistic dreariness. It was so much too large for the settlement, that it appeared to be a very slight improvement on out-doors. It was unpleasantly new.

—A NIGHT AT WINGDAM

Iron-shuttered hotel in Murphy's, Calif., was model for Bret Harte's "Wingdam Temperance Hotel."

and his writing suffered from sudden success. Under the widespread Dickensian influence, his California was peopled wholly by odd characters, and in his eagerness to serve up the expected fare he went in for theatrics rather than truth. In spite of it, his stories breathe some of the early California air and his place in American literature as "father of the Western short story" is secure.

. . . A little beyond . . . a rude cabin, and the claim of Johnson.

Except for the rudest purposes of shelter from rain and cold, the cabin possessed but little advantage over the simple savagery of surrounding nature. . . .

The claim worked by Johnson in his intervals of sobriety was represented by half a dozen rude openings in the mountainside, with the heaped-up débris of rock and gravel before the mouth of each. . . .

—MRS. SKAGGS'S HUSBANDS

An "old claim" still gapes on Jackass Hill where Bret Harte and Mark Twain lived.

Artemus Ward

One of the most popular American humorists, and an accomplished showman in Barnum's age of showmen, was Artemus Ward, a farm boy from Waterford Flat, Maine, whose real name was Charles Farrar Browne.

Trained as a typesetter, Browne gained a small fame as reporter and editor of the Cleveland *Plain Dealer* with fictitious letters from an old Indianan named Artemus Ward who wrote about his carnival, which included "three moral bares, a kangaroo (an amoozing little Raskal) and some wax figgers." Eventually Browne tired of journalism and became a showman himself. His first dodge, in the form of a lecture, was called "Babes in the Woods" and consisted of jests, dry observations on fashions and foibles of mankind, and sarcasms on political and social topics of the day. It was an immediate success and "Artemus Ward" took to the country.

One of his tour stops was Salt Lake City, capital of the then quite aggressive and polygamous Mormons. Due to perform, he was warned by a U. S. Army captain stationed outside town to "see all as if you were not looking and keep your thoughts to yourself." Stricken by illness on arrival, Browne had time to learn several valuable facts—that Brigham Young was synonymous with "The Church," that he was the fountain of all goodness and therefore reserved the right to be reservoir of all riches. He first saw Young at a ball at which apostles, saints, and prophets all danced merrily. When the "lecture" was finally held with full co-operation from the Mormons, Browne noticed to his dismay that most of his jokes went over the saints' heads.

Back in New York, Browne distilled his experiences into a famous lecture, later published as a book, entitled *Artemus Ward among the Mormons*, and advertised it by sending twelve Irishmen disguised as Indians along Broadway. It was a roaring success.

Brigham Young's house in Salt Lake City had gabled rooms for all of his many wives and children.

Nobody seems to know how many wives Brigham Young has. Some set the number as high as eighty, in which case his children must be too numerous to mention. Each wife has a room to herself. These rooms are large and airy, and I suppose they are supplied with all the modern improvements. But never having been invited to visit them, I can't speak very definitely about this. . . .

—BRIGHAM YOUNG

Rude limestone grave of a pioneer on way west marks Oregon Trail near Lewellen, Neb.

Francis Parkman

Young Francis Parkman of Boston in 1846 planned to explore the West, with a friend, with no more serious purpose in mind than a summer's adventure.

The great westward trek across America had just begun, spurred by the doctrine of Manifest Destiny and the widespread publication of Frémont's overland routes to Oregon, California, and Mexico. By 1846 two or three thousand people had set out along the Oregon Trail. Fur trappers' outposts and forts sprang up along the way, one of the most important of them Fort Laramie, named after one Jacques la Ramée, near the North Platte in Wyoming.

Originally a crossroads of the old Indian route that became the Oregon Trail and the north-south route along the front range of the Rockies, Fort Laramie was a trade center for independent trappers and a stopover for thousands of pioneers. Within or without its walls camped mountain men, Indians, gold diggers, Mormons, and soldiers.

When Parkman arrived in June he found that an entire Indian village had pitched its tents outside the adobe walls. He noted in his journal—basis for *The Oregon Trail*—that prices were extortionate: sugar $2.00 a cup, 5-cent tobacco $1.50, bullets 75 cents a pound. The American Fur Company had just begun to freeze out the independent voyageurs and trappers.

It was still many years before Parkman, the wealthy young Bostonian, was to become the great historian of the new West. In 1846 his youthful tendency to ridicule the uncouth emigrant pioneers was too great for him to appreciate their hardships or the profound forces that were changing the West.

Ruins of Fort Laramie, Wyo., form an American "Stonehenge" against the setting western sun.

. . . A moment after, the hills seeming to draw apart as we advanced, disclosed Fort Laramie itself, its high bastions and perpendicular walls of clay crowning an eminence on the left beyond the stream . . .

—THE OREGON TRAIL

The bent oaks of Grand Isle have withstood the hurricanes and floods of the Gulf of Mexico.

LAFCADIO HEARN

On the Gulf side of these islands you may observe that the trees—when there are any trees—all bend away from the sea; and, even of bright, hot days when the wind sleeps, there is something grotesquely pathetic in their look of agonized terror. A group of oaks at Grand Isle I remember as especially suggestive: five stooping silhouettes in line against the horizon, like fleeing women with streaming garments and wind-blown hair,—bowing grievously and thrusting out arms desperately northward as to save themselves from falling.

—CHITA

Patricio Lafcadio Tessima Carlos Hearn, native of Leucadia in the Ionian Sea and son of an Irish officer and a Maltese mother, came to America at nineteen, a frail, ugly orphan dogged by excessive timidity. He emerged from a miserable life in Cincinnati as a reporter and writer, later moved to New Orleans, where he found some happiness among its exotic, hybrid people. Steeped in Creole lore and Oriental thought, he struck a new note in American writing and his brilliant, extravagant style finally attracted Northern publishers.

The idea for *Chita*, a story of man's battle with the elements, came to him on Grand Isle, where he heard the tragedy of Last Island, an antebellum resort swept away by a hurricane in 1856. He died in Japan, where his search for the exotic had finally led him.

"Jo! Jo, where are you?" cried Meg, at the foot of the garret stairs.

"Here!" answered a husky voice from above; and, running up, Meg found her sister eating apples and crying over the "Heir of Redclyffe," wrapped up in a comforter on an old three-legged sofa by the sunny window. This was Jo's favorite refuge; and here she loved to retire with half a dozen russets and a nice book, to enjoy the quiet and the society of a pet rat who lived near by, and didn't mind her a particle.

—LITTLE WOMEN

LOUISA MAY ALCOTT

Little Women was the book of the year for 1868. The first question asked of commuters on their way "downtown" to Boston was, "Have you read it yet?" But not only around Boston was it a best seller: the transcontinental railroad, completed that year, carried it quickly across the continent and made it a national success. Its appeal was not regional, since it told the story with simplicity and reality of what could be any American family.

For Louisa it had been a long struggle. Second daughter of the impecunious Transcendentalist pedagogue Bronson Alcott, little Louisa, like her counterpart Jo, developed into the family tomboy but still found time for stories and sentimental poems. After a nomadic childhood in and around Boston, the constantly poor but high-minded Alcotts settled for a time in Concord. Here at Hillside (now Wayside) Louisa spent those "happiest years of my life," from thirteen to sixteen, that were the basis for *Little Women.*

As a girl she had made up her mind to forego marriage (which she considered a "trap" anyway) for a writing career which might help out her family. Finally established at Orchard House in Concord, she wrote dozens of sketches, stories, poems, and plays, and achieved moderate success as an author. This was interrupted by a brief career as a Civil War nurse in Washington, where the unaccustomed impact of pain, sex, and death was too much for her high-strung nature and she suffered a nervous breakdown.

When her publisher approached her with the idea of a girls' story she was not enthusiastic, but she had always wanted to write about the family, and had even chosen the working title "The Pathetic Family." Her book is still a perennial seller the world over, and her home is a national shrine.

Attic in Orchard House took the place for Louisa of "Jo's" garret as favorite reading and writing nook.

A star over Louisa's grave in Concord, Mass., cemetery commemorates her service as a Civil War nurse.

Sarah Orne Jewett

As Sarah Orne Jewett drove the rounds with her doctor father through the decaying harbors and salt-water farms of southern Maine, she saw that the sun was setting on her New England and tried to capture its atmosphere as it looked to her in the romantic light of a vanishing past. There is a "hint of glory departed" in her stories and sketches, while her descriptions of locale are meticulously factual.

Descendant of sea captains and merchants whose mansions recall Cavalier rather than Puritan days, Sarah loved her Maine coasts and defended her countrymen against "city boarders" who thought them ignorant. Long on background, short on plot, her stories had a remarkable purity of style, and, unlike other mourners of fading New England, she had no despair in her tone, no falling back upon the grotesque or the coarse. In *Deephaven* and *The Country of the Pointed Firs* she painted in Irvingesque manner "the present upon the background of the past."

Today Sarah Orne Jewett is best remembered as forerunner of such writers as Willa Cather, whom she once laughingly told that her head was full of old houses and old women and that when the two got together in her brain with a click, she knew a story was under way.

Decaying harbor of York, Me., like "Deephaven," once boasted busy wharves and fleets of sailing vessels.

Hamilton House, mirrored in Piscataqua River near South Berwick, Me., was scene of *The Tory Lover*.

The last day of October in 1777, Colonel Jonathan Hamilton came out of his high house on the river bank with a handsome, impatient company of guests, all Berwick gentlemen.

—THE TORY LOVER

. . . the Panamint hills were already but blue hummocks on the horizon. Before him . . . stretched primordial desolation. League upon league the infinite reaches of dazzling white alkali laid themselves out like an immeasurable scroll unrolled from horizon to horizon; not a bush, not a twig relieved that horrible monotony. . . . It was abominable, this hideous sink of alkali, this bed of some primeval lake lying so far below the level of the ocean.

—MCTEAGUE

FRANK NORRIS

"The Dentist," as Norris referred to his first novel *McTeague,* was started during the author's year at Harvard and finished at the Big Dipper Mine in the California Sierras. When it appeared in 1899—a year after *When Knighthood Was in Flower*— most reviewers called it "a strong book, bordering on the scandalous," and urged Norris to eschew his naturalism in favor of American "idealism." Only Howells praised it as a step forward, but Norris is now generally credited with having first brought naturalism to American literature.

Frank Norris was a Chicagoan who as an art student had tasted the Left Bank bohemian life of Paris but was mostly interested in French medieval romances. Only later, when he returned to San Francisco, did he come under the influence of Zola and the new naturalistic trend. He never achieved the objectivity necessary to the true naturalist, nor was he exclusively interested in determinism. The individual, "the raw man, the man with his shirt off, stripped to the buff and fighting for his life," was his chief concern. As he matured as a writer this concern developed into a consideration of man in a struggle with social forces, but his sudden death at thirty-two cut short his ambitious plans for a trilogy on America showing the interplay of natural and industrial forces, and only two of the novels, *The Octopus* and *The Pit,* appeared.

The arid salt and alkali flats extend for miles in

Death Valley where Norris's hero McTeague met his melodramatic end.

A one-room Indiana school like this one at Hebron inspired Eggleston's *The Hoosier Schoolmaster.*

EDWARD EGGLESTON

Edward Eggleston is one of the rough-hewn pioneers without whom American realistic fiction wouldn't have broken through the idyllic fog of romantic gentility as soon as it did. A native of southern Indiana, he had been teacher, preacher, Bible agent, traveling salesman, soapmaker, showman, and journalist, and though he wrote dozens of other books, *The Hoosier Schoolmaster* was the one that brought him national fame.

Based on his knowledge of teaching in the backwoods Ohio River region, it is a hilariously funny tale of the troubles of a young teacher among the Pennsylvania Dutch and Hoosiers who clung to the "no lickin' no larnin' " school of pedagogy but whose children could often beat up the master. Published in 1871, the book was an immediate sensation, and so many copies were pirated abroad that Eggleston also became a pioneer in international copyright—his book was among the first to appear under the new law of 1891.

"Want to be a school-master, do you? . . . Why, the boys have driv off the last two, and licked the one afore them like blazes. . . . They'd pitch you out of doors, sonny, neck and heels, afore Christmas. . . . Howsumdever, ef you think you kin trust your hide in Flat Crick school-house I ha'n't got no 'bjection. But ef you git licked, don't come on us. Flat Crick don't pay no 'nsurance, you bet!". . .

—THE HOOSIER SCHOOLMASTER

Ambrose Bierce

The battle for Kennesaw Mountain was one of the hottest in the Georgia campaign of the Civil War. For a day it raged around the wooded slopes of the hill, and among the many Union casualties was First Lieutenant Ambrose Bierce, topographical officer, who received a musket ball through his head. Bierce got over the physical wound, but the war left him with a psychological scar forever. Years later the Kennesaw incident appeared in *One of the Missing*, in his book *Tales of Soldiers and Civilians.*

Born in an Ohio log cabin of Connecticut parents, Bierce went to San Francisco after the war, and from free lancing rose to star writer on young Hearst's *Examiner* and was the literary dictator of the West Coast. "Bitter Bierce" kept politicians, hypocrites, and pious stuffed shirts of all sorts worried with his vitriolic pen.

He wrote stories for his own entertainment, earning his living through the "abuse" of journalism, as he called it. Set down with restraint and no trace of moralizing, his grim tales first caught on in France and England—his interest in death and the supernatural and his bitter satire kept him from being popular in American literary circles until after World War I: a period of greater sophistication as well as disillusion, when he began to be widely appreciated. Bierce disappeared mysteriously in the Mexican revolution of 1914 and no trace of him has ever been found.

. . . Concealing himself in the débris of joists and flooring Searing looked across the open ground between his point of view and a spur of Kennesaw Mountain, a half-mile away. A road leading up and across this spur was crowded with troops—the rear-guard of the retiring enemy, their gun-barrels gleaming in the morning sunlight.

—ONE OF THE MISSING

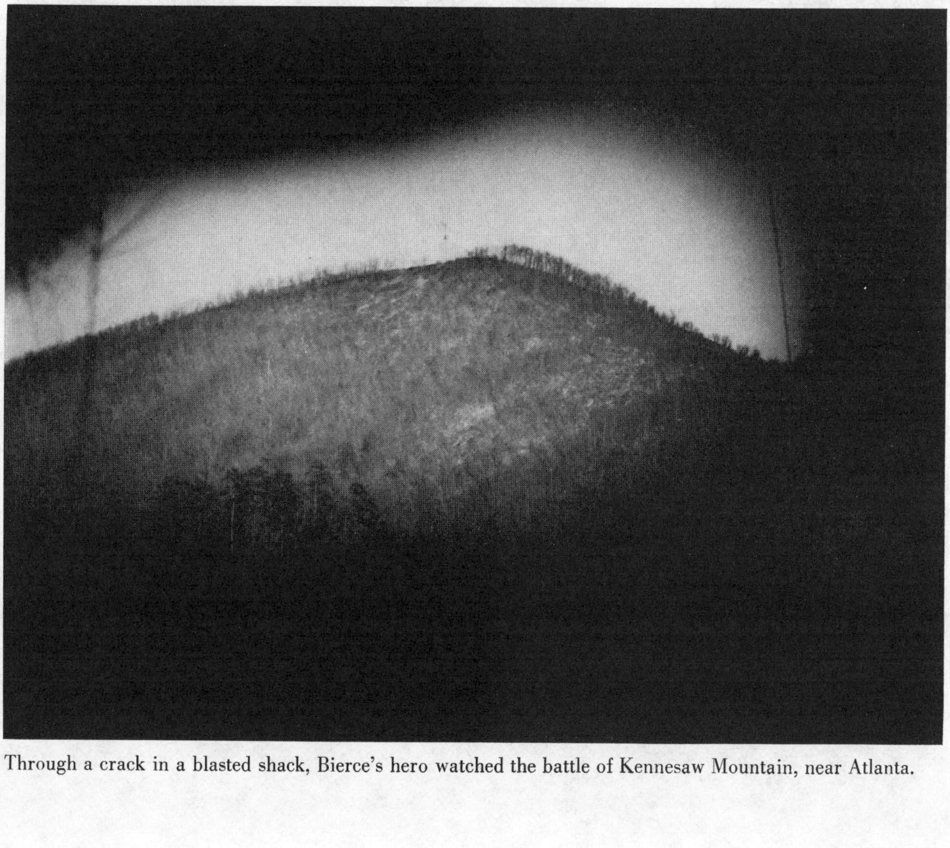

Through a crack in a blasted shack, Bierce's hero watched the battle of Kennesaw Mountain, near Atlanta.

"Lapham" longed for social aura of Beacon Street.

. . . The long procession of lamps on the beautiful street was flaring. . . . Lapham, with a lump in his throat, stopped in front of his house and looked at their multitude. . . . They were a part of his pride and glory, his success, his triumphant life's work which was fading into failure in his helpless hands. He ground his teeth to keep down that lump, but the moisture in his eyes blurred the lamps, and the keen pale crimson against which it made them flicker.

—THE RISE OF SILAS LAPHAM

William Dean Howells

When the hero of William Dean Howells's *The Rise of Silas Lapham* supervised the building of his dream-mansion on Beacon Street, he was looking forward to a residence in the newest, most fashionable Boston neighborhood of the day. Today Beacon Street still holds a certain glamour for some Bostonians, and though many of its narrow-fronted houses have been turned into schools, institutions, or refined boardinghouses, some old families have still managed to cling to their homes with the choice rear view of the boat-studded Charles River Basin.

Silas Lapham's appearance marked the climax of William Dean Howells's Boston period. Its theme was dear to Americans of all eras—that of the rough-and-ready, self-made man whose standards come into conflict with the sophisticated metropolis —and it won an immediate and lasting popularity.

It was no accident that most of Howells's earlier novels dealt with New England. A native of Ohio and a successful young journalist there, he came to his "Holy Land of Boston" like a pilgrim attaining his shrine. As an editor of the *Atlantic Monthly* for fifteen years, he evolved his theory of "selective realism." To him the adjective "realistic" signified democratic, while "romantic" was synonymous with aristocratic. He believed then that the main task of American realism was to steer clear of passion or tragedy and keep to the fate of the average man and "the more smiling aspects of life."

Unfortunately the tastes of an invalid wife and a Midwesterner's awe of New England culture somewhat watered down his "realism" to careful analyses of local conventions, feminine nerves, and endless conversations until he moved to a more cosmopolitan New York. In that new literary capital he came under the liberalizing spell of European scientific and social thought, particularly that of Tolstoi. Now instead of dealing in fragile shades of sophistication he took up, in *Altruria*, *A Hazard of New Fortunes*, and *Through the Eye of the Needle*, the more pressing problems of the day.

Considered a bit old-fashioned nowadays, Howells was nevertheless for sixty years the chief bellwether of an American realistic fiction that is second nature to writers today, and exerted a large and beneficial influence far into the twentieth century.

Boston's Charles River abuts "water side of Beacon."

"Yes, sir, it's about the sightliest view I know of. I always did like the water side of Beacon. Long before I owned property here, or ever expected to, m'wife and I used to ride down this way, and stop the buggy to get this view over the water. When people talk to me about the Hill, I can understand 'em. It's snug, and it's old-fashioned, and it's where they've always lived. But when they talk about Commonwealth Avenue, I don't know what they mean. It don't hold a candle to the water side of Beacon. . . . No, sir! when you come to the Back Bay at all, give me the water side of Beacon."

—THE RISE OF SILAS LAPHAM

A defeated "Maggie," the bright lights of New York behind her, heads for the blackness of the river.

She went into the blackness of the final block. The shutters of the tall buildings were closed like grim lips. . . . Afar off the lights of the avenues glittered as if from an impossible distance. Street-car bells jingled with a sound of merriment. . . .

At the feet of the tall buildings appeared the deathly black hue of the river. . . . The varied sounds of life, made joyous by distance and seeming unapproachableness, came faintly and died away to a silence.

—MAGGIE: A GIRL OF THE STREETS

STEPHEN CRANE

Twenty-one-year-old Stephen Crane was living in a lower East Side boardinghouse in New York when he wrote *Maggie.* A minister's son from Newark, he had been a reporter and had tried some bizarre sketches, but now he felt he wanted to do something different. After rewriting it several times, and having had little luck with publishers, he borrowed $869 and brought out 1,100 copies himself under the pen name of Johnston Smith and no title. The book sold for 50 cents but had few takers. Brentano's returned ten of its twelve copies, and reviewers ignored it with the exception of Hamlin Garland, who called it "graphic, terrible in its directness," and William Dean Howells, who admired its "Greek" sense of inevitability and urged Harper's, in vain, to reprint it. Only later, when Crane had won recognition with his remarkable *The Red Badge of Courage,* was *Maggie* reissued.

Crane held himself an Impressionist who "believed in irony" although some called him "the first American naturalist." His complete detachment, his avoidance of moralizing, and the fatalistic manner in which *Maggie*'s sordid world pressed in on its people made the book unique in American literature, though still totally unacceptable at the time. His influence on such writers as Willa Cather, Hemingway, Dreiser, Sherwood Anderson, Sandburg, Sinclair Lewis, and F. Scott Fitzgerald is nevertheless seen today.

Riley's "Old Swimmin'-Hole" still feels good to the kids of his native Greenfield, Indiana.

JAMES WHITCOMB RILEY

Unlike Garland, who wrote of the broken dreams of the Wisconsin farmer, James Whitcomb Riley extolled the gentler bucolic, folksy Midwest village life.

Native of little Greenfield, in the flat, sunny center of Indiana, Riley grew up on *McGuffey's Readers*, showed an early predilection for the banjo, guitar, fiddle, and drum, and joined a traveling medicine show whose products he helped sell with recitations, from the wagon tailboard, in dialect verse. His first collection appeared under the title of *The Old Swimmin'-Hole and 'Leven Other Poems;* while he was staff poet on the Indianapolis *Journal*, his fame as the Hoosier Bard was established and soon spread beyond Indiana. Schools celebrated special "Riley Days" and the sale of his books was said to outstrip even that of Longfellow's.

Oh! the old swimmin'-hole! whare the crick so still and deep
Looked like a baby-river that was laying half asleep,
And the gurgle of the worter round the drift just below
Sounded like the laugh of something we onc't ust to know . . .

—THE OLD SWIMMIN'-HOLE

Henry James

. . . The apple-tree in New England, plays the part of the olive in Italy, charges itself with the effect of detail, for the most part otherwise too scantly produced, and, engaged in this charming care, becomes infinitely decorative and delicate. . . . Its office in the early autumn is to scatter coral and gold. . . .

—THE AMERICAN SCENE

New York and Boston were two American cities that meant something special to Henry James, who spent most of his mature life away from America. He wrote several tales about each, *The Bostonians* and *Washington Square* among them, and left brilliant pictures of both cities as he remembered them from an earlier day. Early, pre-industrial New York he particularly recalled from his own childhood, much of it spent near his birthplace on Washington Place off the Square.

Washington Square was a tight little society, he noted later in his memoirs, screened in conveniently to the north and west but open wide to the east and comparatively so to the south. Broadway, from Union Square to Barnum's Museum by City Hall, was its main attraction. Brownstone had just become fashionable, and many of the neighboring houses "affronted the day" with it. Altogether the world of the Square seemed to him, in retrospect, to have been one of "quieter harmonies . . . so decent in its dignity, so instinctively unpretentious." Today,

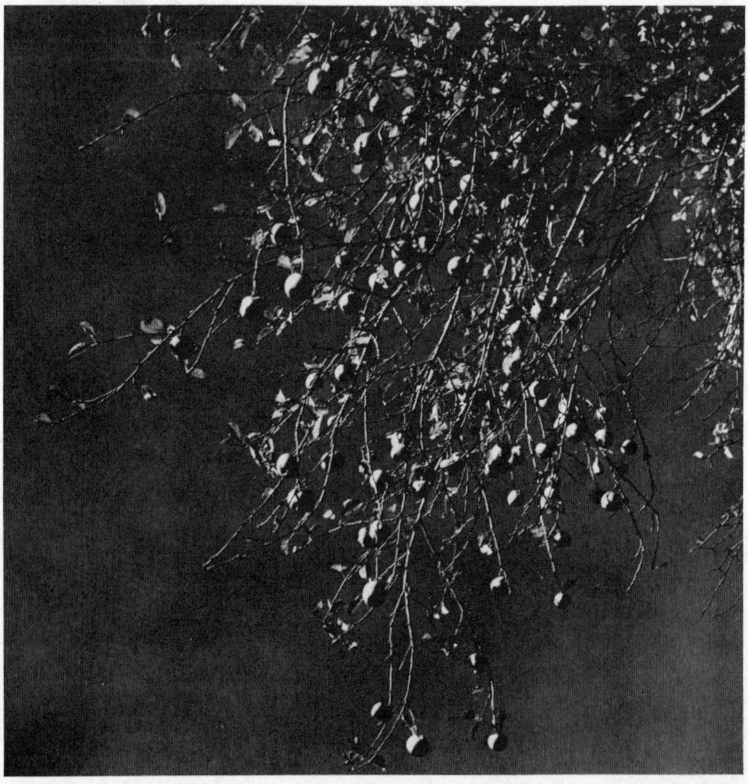

The red and gold apples of New England delighted James after many years in Europe.

James heiress, "Catherine Sloper," lived in a Washington Square mansion.

the Square and its shady park still offer the chief recreation for the neighborhood, but many of the old houses are beginning to come down, one by one.

After an absence of twenty-one years in Europe, James returned to find New York changed, "appalling, phantastically charmless and dire," as he recalled in *The American Scene.* A refugee from an industrial America who had been taught to worship culture since childhood, he chose to study the subtleties of European society and to absorb himself in psychological probings (his famous brother William was a founder of scientific psychology). In this double pursuit, Henry James stands as the last Victorian romantic and at the same time an all-important forerunner of the modern psychological novel.

The ideal of quiet and of genteel retirement, in 1835, was found in Washington Square, where the Doctor built himself a handsome, modern, wide-fronted house, with . . . a flight of white marble steps ascending to a portal which was also faced with white marble. This structure, and many of its neighbors, which it exactly resembled, were supposed, forty years ago to embody the last results of architectural science, and they remain to this day very solid and honorable dwellings. In front of them was the square, containing a considerable quantity of inexpensive vegetation . . . and round the corner was the more august precinct of the Fifth Avenue, taking its origin at this point with a spacious and confident air which already marked it for high destinies. . . .

—WASHINGTON SQUARE

"Land's End," onetime Wharton residence, was among fashionable "cottages" along Newport rocks.

But the Wellands always went to Newport, where they owned one of the square boxes on the cliffs, and their son-in-law could adduce no good reason why he and May should not join them there. As Mrs. Welland rather tartly pointed out, it was hardly worth while for May to have worn herself out trying on summer clothes in Paris if she was not to be allowed to wear them.

—THE AGE OF INNOCENCE

. . . "Ethan! Ethan! I want you to take me down again!"

"Down where?"

"The coast. Right off," she panted. "So't we'll never come up any more.". . .

She put her lips close against his ear to say: "Right into the big elm. You said you could. So't we'd never have to leave each other any more."

—ETHAN FROME

EDITH WHARTON

Edith Wharton, like many another daughter of fashionable New York, spent most of her girlhood summers in Newport, R. I., when she was not traveling abroad. Even after her marriage she continued on there for some years, in a house of her own, "Land's End," at the lower end of the cliff walk where the waves beat ceaselessly on the rocky ledge and some friends felt the elemental setting ill attuned to her elegant urbanity. A brilliant hostess and an authority on interior decoration, Mrs. Wharton eventually deserted Newport for the gentle Berkshire country and lived for many years in her Lenox mansion, "The Mount," now a school.

Daughter of one of New York's best families, and of a mother who could recite the names of the "Four Hundred" in order of rank, she had the perfect manners of a model young lady. She also had, fortunately for literary posterity, an acute and searching intelligence which turned her to writing. Most of her legacy of forty books in forty-five years is concerned with her three principles of culture, class, and morality.

For her Pulitzer prize-winning social satire, *The Age of Innocence*, Edith Wharton drew easily on her wide knowledge of earlier New York and Newport society. But in *Ethan Frome* she stepped out of her milieu to write a brilliant, almost operatic, tour de force about inarticulate New England farm people.

A student of the analytical style of her friend Henry James, she was, like him, so at home in the older and more established European society, particularly that of the Faubourg St.-Germain, that she could smile at its poor provincial, transient American counterpart.

A lamppost stands at foot of Courthouse Hill in Lenox, Mass., where "Ethan" and "Matt" coasted.

Fields of corn and velvety Wisconsin meadows still spread around the Garland homestead in Green's Coulee.

HAMLIN GARLAND

Another champion of realism seeking to purge American literature of its lingering romanticism was Hamlin Garland, a son of the Middle Border. Child of homesteaders ever moving west, he spent his early days on a farm in the beautiful Wisconsin coulee still remembered by neighbors as the "Garland Place" and by him as a "delightful place for boys."

Like his fellow-Midwesterner Howells, he had gone to Boston as "a passionate pilgrim in search of richer culture." There he taught, wrote for reformist journals, and added Spencerian evolutionary ideas to his early agnosticism, steeping himself in the European naturalists, in Whitman, and in Howells. It was when he returned to his boyhood home that he was struck by the spiritual and economic barrenness of American farm life, caught as it was in the throes of depression and a losing struggle with the railroads and financial interests of the East. In *Main-Travelled Roads* he wrote of the contrast he saw between the rich beauty of the land and the gracelessness of the farmers' lives—a phase of rural existence the idyllic writers had theretofore neglected.

Our farm lay well up what is called Green's coulee in a little valley just over the road which runs along the LaCrosse river in western Wisconsin. It contained one hundred sixty acres of land which crumpled against the wooded hills on the east and lay well upon a ridge to the west . . . over the height to the north was the land of the red people, and small bands of their hunters used occasionally to come trailing down across our meadow . . .

—A SON OF THE MIDDLE BORDER

Gently rolling pastures and fields have supplanted the barren, forbidding South Dakota prairies.

Ole Rölvaag

Rölvaag's father-in-law was one of the earliest settlers of the rolling Sioux Valley prairies of South Dakota, where vast farms and rich harvests today belie the terrifying desert loneliness of a hundred years ago. He had come just after the Civil War and had followed the route from Minnesota that Per Hansa, hero of *Giants in the Earth,* was to take. Like Per Hansa, he settled not far from Colton, near the Iowa border, and cut his first sod hut out of the black prairie earth.

Norwegian-born Rölvaag saw in the homesteading Per Hansa and his tiny band of countrymen the conquering spirit of the pioneer whose vision of the promised land makes him stronger with each new struggle. In Hansa's wife Beret, though, he saw Old World civilization with its fears and longings, its gloomy religious fatalism, and old Norse superstition which made her shrink from the prairie's challenge and finally succumb. Written in Norwegian and later translated, *Giants* invests the thoroughly American theme of frontier conquest with the rich tradition of Scandinavian literature.

. . . . *This formless prairie had no heart that beat, no waves that sang, no soul that could be touched. . . .*

The infinitude surrounding her on every hand might not have been so oppressive, might even have brought her a measure of peace, if it had not been for the deep silence, which lay heavier here than in a church. . . .

—GIANTS IN THE EARTH

General store in Croydon, N. H., proudly bears the name of Churchill's novel.

WINSTON CHURCHILL

. . . Across the road is Jonah Winch's store, with a platform so high that a man may step off his horse directly on to it; with its checker-paned windows, with its dark interior smelling of coffee and apples and molasses, yes, and of Endea rum—for this was before the days of the revivals. . . .

—CONISTON

Winston Churchill (no relation to Britain's Prime Minister) was a Missourian by birth and a New Hampshireman by choice. His writing career began with historical romances such as *The Crisis* and the enormously popular *Richard Carvel,* which sold more than 1,000,000 copies; and, though he stopped writing in 1917, he was still in 1924 "one of the greatest writers" of the twentieth century.

A member of the New Hampshire legislature and Progressive candidate for governor, Churchill as a disciple of "trust-busting" Theodore Roosevelt was a literary reformer, and in the so-called "muckraking" era inveighed against the evils of monopoly and machine politics. Prototype for his rural political boss in *Coniston* was a man named Ruel Durkee, still remembered by local people, who will point out his house from the steps of the general store in Croydon.

Old N. Y. Police Headquarters, once Steffens's beat, is now a court.

LINCOLN STEFFENS

Without experience but with obvious journalistic talents, young Lincoln Steffens as financial reporter on E. L. Godkin's reformist New York *Evening Post* soon mastered the intricacies of Wall Street and was switched to police headquarters, an unusual departure for the unsensational *Post.* Here, under the guidance of Jacob Riis, he turned to social questions and, when Teddy Roosevelt was made one of three new police commissioners, served with Riis on a "kitchen cabinet" exposing widespread corruption "on the force."

He went on to put "muckraking" on a national basis as editor of *McClure's,* with Ray Stannard Baker and Ida M. Tarbell. Later, as a semiofficial diplomatic representative of the U. S. under Wilson, he kept his reporter's skepticism and his reformer's enthusiasm. His *The Shame of the Cities* and *Autobiography* are today classics for anyone interested in public affairs.

. . . The Post *had never had a man in Mulberry Street, where the heads of the police and detective services had their offices. It was the source of crime news. . . . I went to police headquarters as I had gone to Wall Street, as I had gone to Europe, and as I had come home to America, with the suppressed ardor of a young student and with the same throbbing anxiety that an orator feels just before he rises to speak.*

—THE AUTOBIOGRAPHY OF LINCOLN STEFFENS

. . . I knew every inch of the way. Once a writer friend of mine had owned the ranch; but he, too, had become a revolutionist, though more disastrously than I, for he was already dead and gone, and none knew where nor how. He alone, in the days he had lived, knew the secret of the hiding-place for which I was bound.

—THE IRON HEEL

JACK LONDON

Jack London was describing his own Sonoma Valley place when he wrote in *The Iron Heel* of the Socialist hideout on "the ranch of a writer friend." He had bought the ranch in 1905 "for beauty" and too high a price, and local farmers predicted he would never make six per cent on it. He never did. The ranch was a bottomless pit into which most of London's earnings poured, through fabulous projects invariably ending in disaster. The worst was the $70,000 "Wolf House," which took three years to build and burned down as he was about to move in.

London the ranch owner and successful author was a far cry from the poor boy of Oakland. Born in the depression of the seventies, child of an astrologer and a spiritualist, he had undergone every imaginable privation by the time he was twenty. He had worked in a cannery at 10 cents an hour per twenty-hour day, reigned as "Prince of the Oyster Pirates" in San Francisco Bay, shipped to the Far East, worked in a jute mill, followed Coxey's Army, and prospected in the Klondike. Out of it emerged an avid seeker for knowledge, an aspiring writer, and a Socialist. His first stories caught on after a few years of failure and *The Call of the Wild* and *The Sea Wolf* finally brought him the financial success he craved. In the growing Socialist Party under Eugene Debs he was a chief speaker and propagandist, and *The Iron Heel* was his literary contribution to the cause. Written in 1907, it became an extraordinary prophecy of the twentieth century, with its predictions of the rise of fascism, a feat noted by Anatole France in his introduction to an edition issued in 1924, following Mussolini's seizure of power.

An erratic writer who later turned out frequently melodramatic potboilers, London is remembered for his adventure yarns, for brilliant, intense short stories, and as one of the earliest writers dealing with the lives of working people and major problems of his age.

"The Valley of the Moon," Jack London's Cali-

fornia ranch, stretches along the wooded Sonoma Mountain.

Adams house in Quincy stands in quiet eighteenth-century elegance amid profusion of shrubs and flowers.

HENRY ADAMS

The two houses in which Henry Adams spent many years of his life—his ancestral house in Quincy, Mass., and the one he built on Lafayette Square in Washington—were two symbolic poles of his life. Neither ever quite satisfied him.

Though born near Boston's State Street, he grew up in the atmosphere of Quincy, which (as he wrote in his *Education*) "belonged to a different world. The old house at Quincy was eighteenth century. What style it had was in its Queen Anne mahogany panels and its Louis Seize chairs and sofas." Both can be admired today by anyone curious to see the home of two Presidents and of the brilliant Adams dynasty, now a well-preserved national shrine.

Equipped with an eighteenth-century rational mind, an inheritance of Adams integrity, and a bent for disinterested criticism, Henry Adams set about adapting himself to the maelstrom of post-Civil War America. Neither diplomacy, finance, nor teaching medieval history at Harvard satisfied him. He moved to Washington, where he became the "stablemate of statesmen," as he euphemistically called Grant, Blaine, Sherman, and Conkling. There, too, he immersed himself in the study of early American politics and produced brilliant histories of the Jefferson-Madison period; but again in dissatisfaction found his outlook too narrowly political and felt he would have to re-educate himself. He turned to Darwinian biology and to physics in search of a suitable philosophy, but force and determinism alone did not suit, and he looked further for a view that would reconcile determinism and progress and show him a unity in multiplicity. He found it in the two centuries of the Middle Ages that were overshadowed by the spirit of Mont St.-Michel and then of Chartres Cathedral—two periods representing to him the highest points yet achieved by human aspiration.

So Adams, an honest man with a critical mind, sat on in Washington, looking down on the heroes of the American past, casting about for a more humane mode of life than the "bankers' paradise" that had replaced his earlier, simpler world of Quincy.

Adams's second home looked out on Lafayette Sq., the White House, and Washington Monument.

Hay and Adams had the advantage of looking out of their windows on the antiquities of La Fayette Square, with the sense of having all that any one had; all that the world had to offer; all that they wanted in life. . . . Their chief title to consideration was their right to look out of their windows on great men, alive or dead, in La Fayette Square, a privilege which had nothing to do with their writings.

—THE EDUCATION OF HENRY ADAMS

Purple sage and dwarf cedars carpet the vast upland Utah deserts north of the Grand Canyon.

. . . Her clear sight intensified the purple sage-slope as it rolled before her. . . . Dark, lonely cedar-trees, few and far between, stood out strikingly, and at long distances ruins of red rocks. . . . Northward the slope descended to a dim line of cañons from which rose an up-flinging of the earth, not mountainous, but a vast heave of purple uplands, with ribbed and fan-shaped walls, castle-crowned cliffs, and gray escarpments. . . .

—RIDERS OF THE PURPLE SAGE

ZANE GREY

Ever since the days of Bret Harte, stories about heroes and desperadoes of the West have been staple local and export items of American literary fare. Of the numberless writers to take advantage of the demand, Zane Grey, onetime ballplayer and dentist, was king. Of his fifty-four novels (not all Westerns) twenty-five of them written in seventeen years had a sale of 17,000,000. *Riders of the Purple Sage*, accepted with reluctance by his publishers, ran to 1,000,000 copies and 800,000 reprints. It was based on a Western trip that Grey made in 1908, during which he stayed in Kanab, Utah, now a favorite spot for movie Westerns, but then a rich source of information about the Mormons and their early efforts at colonization. Whatever may be said of their literary quality, two things about his books are certain: they fulfilled the dreams of millions of city-dwellers back East, and their sun-drenched backgrounds have the color and authority of a writer familiar with his country.

On his bench in Madison Square Soapy moved uneasily. When wild geese honk high of nights, and when women without sealskin coats grow kind to their husbands, and when Soapy moves uneasily on his bench in the park, you may know that winter is near at hand.

A dead leaf fell in Soapy's lap. . . .

—THE COP AND THE ANTHEM

O. HENRY

Around the turn of the century a small, shy man strolled the streets of New York from Hell's Kitchen to the Bowery, observing by day and by night the people on the sidewalks, in the parks, restaurants, bars, back rooms, and tenderloin resorts. He was William Sydney Porter, and his walks turned into stories about the "four million" who lived in his "Little Bagdad on the Subway."

A modest, whimsical, ultra-reserved man, reticent about his past, O. Henry lived for years at 55 Irving Place, convenient to a favorite saloon and to an equally favorite park bench in Madison Square.

A native of Greensboro, N. C., he started as a drug clerk, became a Texas cowboy, then a bank clerk. This last got him into financial trouble which resulted in three years in the penitentiary. While still serving time, he sold a story to *McClure's* under his now famous pen name, and his career as the most popular American short-story writer was launched. Later he was special reporter on the New York *World* and a legendary figure in newspaper and literary circles, gathering yarns wherever he went, but never with obvious intent, never with notebook in hand. He once said he had to have a story complete in his mind before he could write it down.

He was most famous for his stories about New York though he wrote widely of the rest of America, and his slangy tales, with their small-town approach and surprise twist at the end, were just right for the tired Gothamite hurrying home with his paper after a hectic day. Though five million O. Henry books have been sold and translations have appeared in most languages, including Chinese and Japanese, critics have lamented his influence on succeeding generations; yet there is no doubt that to the world his name is the symbol of the American short story.

A lonely man sits in Madison Square Park.

UPTON SINCLAIR

Young Upton Sinclair was a poverty-stricken, would-be writer living in the woods near Princeton, N. J., when he took a seven-week trip to Chicago to gather material for the book on "Packingtown" that became a milestone in American literature and history.

The Jungle, first serialized in the Socialist paper *The Appeal to Reason*, told the fate of immigrants living and working in the stockyard area, their struggle to find and keep a job, and to bring up a family in the midst of brutal exploitation. Publishers refused to accept the manuscript without drastic changes, and Jack London, writing in the *Appeal* that it was the "Uncle Tom's Cabin of wage slavery," helped raise $5,000 in order to bring it out. Later reissued commercially, the book marked the climax of the "muckraking" era, and at twenty-eight Sinclair was a national figure and $30,000 richer. The furor prompted a congressional investigation, but a counterfight by the packers resulted

A square mile of stockyards in South Chicago is still the heart of "Packingtown" of Sinclair's *The Jun-*

. . . North and south as far as the eye can reach there stretches a sea of pens. And they were all filled—so many cattle no one had ever dreamed existed in the world. Red cattle, black, white and yellow cattle; old cattle and young cattle; great bellowing bulls and little calves not an hour born; meek-eyed milch cows and fierce, long-horned Texas steers. The sound of them here was as of all the barnyards of the universe. . . .

"By tonight," Jokubas answered, "they will all be killed and cut up."

—THE JUNGLE

only in a pure-food law that left the deplorable conditions as they were until the growth of a labor union and a second investigation in World War I brought a change. Disappointed, Sinclair said he had "aimed at the public's heart and hit its stomach."

gle. Since that novel was written, however, much of America's cattle market has moved farther west.

Old Sangamon County Courthouse in Springfield, Ill., was scene of many an early Lincoln speech.

As in Lindsay's poem, children still gather in the dooryard of Abe Lincoln's pre–White House home.

It is portentous, and a thing of state
That here at midnight, in our little town
A mourning figure walks, and will not rest,
Near the old court-house pacing up and down,

Or by his homestead, or in shadowed yards
He lingers where his children used to play,
Or through the market, on the well-worn stones
He stalks until the dawn-stars burn away.

—ABRAHAM LINCOLN WALKS AT MIDNIGHT

VACHEL LINDSAY

Springfield, "the mystic, where I always live, wherever I may be," and its first citizen Abe Lincoln, always meant something special to Vachel Lindsay. He was born in Lincoln's sister-in-law's house, where the farewell reception had taken place before the President departed for Washington. His uncle lived next door to Lincoln's house, whose rooms and memorabilia young Vachel knew intimately.

A bizarre, wandering apostle of art and beauty, Lindsay set out to be an artist but turned to poetry in search of a "New Christian art." Verse, he decided, must somehow be brought to the common people who otherwise "abhorred it." To that end he evolved a new style, to be delivered in half-sung verse with an emphasis on rhythm. National recognition came to him in 1913, with a *Poetry* Magazine prize for his *General William Booth Enters into Heaven.*

A mystic humanitarian and Christian Socialist with a missionary zeal inherited from his Campbellite parents, he wandered through America declaiming his poetry and spreading his gospel of democracy, beauty, and holiness. Through it he believed that industry-thwarted Americans would turn into a new race.

The "Bridgepoint" railyards fascinated Gertrude Stein's Melanctha, who used to wander down there to watch.

Gertrude Stein

Three Lives, a study of three women of whom "Melanctha" was one, signaled the arrival of a new literary influence. One of her more readable books, it clearly pointed to Gertrude Stein's chief aim: "to get to the very core of the communication of the intuition." She got from William James a concern for the meaning of words and essayed greater clarity and reality through a novel use of them. Alice B. Toklas, her lifelong companion, said that *Three Lives*, "compounded of phrase upon phrase," was affected by the technique of successive brush strokes on a Cézanne painting hanging in front of the author while she wrote.

Gertrude Stein has been called "the fountainhead of all young Americans writing in Paris" in the early decades of this century and many of our most vigorous and today well-established writers served their apprenticeship there.

Melanctha liked to wander, and to stand by the railroad yard, and watch the men and the engines and the switches and everything that was busy there, working. Railroad yards are a ceaseless fascination.

—MELANCTHA

Gardiner, Maine, was the poet's "Tilbury Town."

Old Eben Flood, climbing alone one night
Over the hill between the town below
And the forsaken upland hermitage
That held as much as he should ever know
On earth again of home, paused warily.
The road was his with not a native near;
And Eben, having leisure, said aloud,
For no man else in Tilbury Town to hear:
"Well, Mr. Flood, we have the harvest moon
Again, and we may not have many more;
The bird is on the wing, the poet says,
And you and I have said it here before . . ."

—MR. FLOOD'S PARTY

EDWIN ARLINGTON ROBINSON

"Eben Flood," one of Edwin Arlington Robinson's many "Tilbury" townspeople, is perhaps the best example of that poet's singular personality and art. Based on a story heard in his youth about an elderly Maine eccentric who drank lonely toasts to himself when all his friends had died, *Mr. Flood's Party* is a well-balanced blend of narrative and landscape, lyricism, irony, pathos, and humor—all attributes of the poet's well-known aura of resignation and decay.

Robinson's life, like his muse, was overshadowed by gloom. He was brought up with the deserted mansions and rotting wharves of the old Kennebec River towns, and had daily intercourse with the lonely and defeated old men and women left behind in the great exodus to the cities and to the West. A sensitive man, preoccupied with fear of failure and poverty, he lived a nightmare existence in New York which even Theodore Roosevelt's presidential patronage of his first collected poems could not alleviate. Otherwise ignored, until the poetry "revival" of the second decade, when *Man Against the Sky* and his later Arthurian legends got wider notice, he found a haven at last with other writers and artists in the MacDowell Colony near Jaffrey, N. H.

Robinson was a modern poet of no specific school who strove for greater realism and the use of everyday themes. His efforts to trim poetry of its nonessentials and of the "red-bellied robin" brand of poetic language made him a trail blazer of modern American verse.

Old ships' hulks rot in deserted Maine harbor.

. . . Never a silence like this now
On ships and wharves and water could have been
Since moving time began. He had come back
Once more to a lost world where all was gone
But ghostly shapes that had no life in them,
And to the wrong world he would once have left
By the wrong door. . . .

—AMARANTH

A dead apple tree, young when Frost first knew it, stands in his former orchard.

Robert Frost's first farm in Derry, N. H., is now called "Frosty Acres."

Robert Frost

No orchard's the worse for the wintriest storm;
But one thing about it, it mustn't get warm.
"How often already you've had to be told,
Keep cold, young orchard. Good-bye and keep cold.
Dread fifty above more than fifty below."
I have to be gone for a season or so. . . .
—GOOD-BYE AND KEEP COLD

Like E. A. Robinson, Robert Frost was a trail blazer in American poetry, but unlike him he writes with less despair of his New England. A Californian by birth, it was characteristic of this lover of the countryside to turn his hand to farming when he had to earn a living. But a temperamental reluctance to observe orthodox farming practice (he milked his cows at 10 P.M. to avoid rising at dawn) worked against him, and though he has owned several farms since, they have never been very remunerative.

Frost was saddened by the sight of a deserted home—the tragedy of land going back to wilderness—but he has known also the delights of a ride in the snow, watching a young colt, birches on a hillside, or gathering hay; and a deep, rich humor has helped him over the bitter moments. In factual, natural language he has brought a freshness into American poetry—which until then had been staggering under the load of romantic sentimentality.

Sherwood Anderson

Many small Ohio towns are woven into Sherwood Anderson's *Winesburg, Ohio*, but Clyde, where he spent most of his boyhood, left the strongest impressions. With its white frame houses, its maples and towering elms, it had something of New England about it. Its people were merchants, artisans, lawyers, doctors, and farmers. There were no factories, and the light, sandy loam around town was ideal (and still is) for fruit, corn, wheat, potatoes, and particularly "sauerkraut" cabbage.

The Andersons were poor, and moved from one "haunted" house to another—rent-free because the owners felt that the Andersons would take the "haunt" out. Father was a gay, adventurous ne'er-do-well, and seven children learned early to help an overworked Mrs. Anderson to support the family. Sherwood was the most ambitious, and his passion for tackling any job he could get earned him the town nickname of "Jobby."

His hustling drove him right on through his succeeding years as race-track follower, factory hand, and soldier, until one day he found himself president of a paint factory with a family and the financial security he had craved. Then, just as suddenly, President Anderson walked out of his plant and his family, never to return—convinced, he said, that the "dollar ideal" by which he had been living was a false one and that he could live more creatively by writing.

After some minor books he scored a major success with *Winesburg*, a collection of grotesque portraits that examined the subtle relationships among his people, their ineptitude at expressing themselves, their loneliness and frustration. They were distortions, but since their vagaries were merely enlargements of tendencies present in all of us they had an air of universality. *Winesburg* was called an honest, imaginative, penetrating picture of American town life under the growing impact of industrialism, and though its author remained eternally baffled by the frustrations he wrote about, his was a positive influence on writers of the early twenties, whose search for a richer life was an accurate reflection of postwar America.

Anderson as a boy fished in Raccoon Creek near Clyde, Ohio, his "Winesburg."

Old-timers still line "Winesburg's" Main Street.

. . . He went into Main Street and sat on the curbing before Wracker's tobacco store. For an hour he lingered about listening to the talk of men, but it did not interest him much and he slipped away.
—WINESBURG, OHIO

Rich Nebraska wheat harvests have replaced the red prairie grass that Willa Cather knew as a child.

The Divide is now thickly populated. The rich soil yields heavy harvests; the dry, bracing climate and the smoothness of the land make labor easy for men and beasts. . . . The grain is so heavy that it bends toward the blade and cuts like velvet.

—O PIONEERS!

WILLA CATHER

Few American writers have equaled Willa Sibert Cather in understanding the violent clash that occurred in America when the gentle, hopeful immigrants from the Old World struck the rigorous, inhospitable prairies of the New. To her, it was an eternal preoccupation, and with it she fashioned the greatest of her retrospective novels, *O Pioneers!* and *My Ántonia*, and with little difficulty transposed it to fit the life of a cultured French priest set down in a primitive New Mexico desert (*Death Comes for the Archbishop*) and a seventeenth-century French count and his retinue exiled on the icy cliffs of new Quebec (*Shadows on the Rock*).

A woman of temperament so strong that it conditioned her pioneer heroines, Willa was brought to the flat Nebraska wastes from a lush Virginia farm in 1883. She grew up something of a tomboy among immigrant Czech, German, French, Scandinavian, and Russian neighbors and native American townspeople of bustling Red Cloud. Many of them found their way into her books. While still at the University she did critical pieces for a local newspaper, took a job later in Pittsburgh on the

Annie Pavelka of Bladen, Neb., Willa Cather's lifelong friend, was the model for her *My Ántonia.*

Deserted Nebraska farmhouse recalls the "Forrester place" of *A Lost Lady.*

short-lived *Home Monthly*, and taught school. Eventually she was brought east by *McClure's* magazine and soon became its managing editor.

Cather's consequential writing did not begin till thirty years after she had left the prairie, but her memory was so precise that her early years and friendships came alive again in vivid and loving detail. *One of Ours*—the story of a sensitive boy (probably her cousin George) who was better off dead as a war hero than alive in the petty toils of Webster County—won a Pulitzer prize in 1922. Cather went her own way adhering to no school, romantic or naturalist. She believed in the "unfurnished novel" and painstakingly excluded all but the essentials, which she set down in sparse but invariably luminous style.

The Forrester place, as every one called it, was not at all remarkable; the people who lived there made it seem much larger and finer than it was. . . . It was encircled by porches, too narrow for modern notions of comfort, supported by the fussy, fragile pillars of that time, when every honest stick of timber was tortured by the turning-lathe into something hideous. Stripped of its vines and denuded of its shrubbery, the house would probably have been ugly enough.

—A LOST LADY

Old Richmond homes recall post-bellum days of Glasgow's novels.

Ellen Glasgow

What Willa Cather did for the Midwest pioneer, and Edith Wharton for Eastern "Society," Ellen Glasgow did for the South. Taken as a whole, her novels are a social history of middle-class Virginia from post–Civil War days to modern times; her text is the clashing of the old against the new, agriculture against industry, the Virginia gentleman against the democratic upstart.

Ellen Glasgow, like Cather and Wharton, could speak with authority about the society she described, for she came of old Virginia families deeply rooted in their code of manners and tradition. Influenced by her study of Tolstoi and Dostoievsky, she developed a skeptical attitude and a fine irony toward her surroundings. A literary rebel against antebellum custom in her early books, she grew more conciliatory during the twenties and thirties and was always a little out of step and out of literary fashion.

. . . Hill Street, which had once known fashion, and that only yesterday, as old ladies count, had sunk at last into a humble state of decay. Here and there the edges of porches had crumbled; grass was beginning to sprout by the curbstone; and the once comfortable homes had opened their doors to boarders or let their large, high-ceiled rooms to the impoverished relicts of Confederate soldiers. . . .

—LIFE AND GABRIELLA

Edgar Lee Masters

Percy Bysshe Shelley was Masters's disguise for William Cullen Bryant, relative of poet, buried here.

PERCY BYSSHE SHELLEY

. . . At Thompson's Lake the trigger of my gun
Caught in the side of the boat
And a great hole was shot through my heart.
Over me a fond father erected this marble shaft,
On which stands the figure of a woman
Carved by an Italian artist. . . .

—SPOON RIVER ANTHOLOGY

WASHINGTON MCNEELY

Rich, honored by my fellow citizens,
The father of many children, born of a noble mother,
All raised there
In the great mansion-house, at the edge of town.
Note the cedar tree on the lawn!
I sent all the boys to Ann Arbor, all the girls to Rockford,
The while my life went on, getting more riches and honors—
Resting under my cedar tree at evening. . . .

—SPOON RIVER ANTHOLOGY

Old Petersburg, Concord, New Salem, in the Illinois Sangamon River country, and Lewistown on the Spoon River furnished Edgar Lee Masters with the substance for his remarkable *Spoon River Anthology*. From the age of one year he had lived in Petersburg with grandparents whose memory he preserved in some of his noblest anthology portraits. In Lewistown, where his father had gone to practice law, Masters found the New England descendants there more strait-laced than his exuberant Virginians and Kentuckians of Sangamon County.

Lewistown, with its crosscurrents of politics, finance, church, and courthouse, was small-town America in microcosm: to Masters it was the key that unlocked a larger world. Its leading family stemmed from Ossian Ross, whom Masters called "Washington McNeely," and lived in "a brick mansion of some distinction." Another place for memories was nearby Bernadotte, once a thriving mill center for the rich farm country that surrounded it. Today only a few ruins by the placid Spoon recall that it was ever settled.

Patterned on the Greek *Anthology*, Masters's work is a landmark of postwar American naturalism. As John Cowper Powys later wrote, "nowhere else but in America, nowhere else but in the Middle West, could all these outraged, thwarted, frustrated, poisoned human spirits, drawing their lineage from every race in Europe, whirl up out of the dust as they do here with a sound like that sound that made Dante tremble and even Virgil turn pale on the brink of the Inferno."

Lewistown, Ill., was named for Colonel Lewis Ross, son of town's founder and builder of Ross Mansion.

Summer moon casts shadow of ruined mill on Spoon River at once-thriving community of Bernadotte, Ill.

ISAIAH BEETHOVEN

They told me I had three months to live,
So I crept to Bernadotte,
And sat by the mill for hours and hours
Where the gathered waters deeply moving
Seemed not to move:

. . . .

But here by the mill the castled clouds
Mocked themselves in the dizzy water;
And over its agate floor at night
The flame of the moon ran under my eyes . . .

—SPOON RIVER ANTHOLOGY

Sinclair Lewis

Sinclair Lewis's *Main Street*, written in 1920 by the first American novelist to win a Nobel prize, is often regarded as the one piece of fiction to introduce a postwar literary era of debunking.

Lewis himself called the trend best in his Nobel prize speech, when he said that it was not difficult to characterize French and English common folk as one really saw them, but it had not previously occurred to him that "one might without indecency write of the people of Sauk Center, Minnesota, as one felt about them. Our fictional tradition, you see, was that all of us in Midwestern villages were altogether noble and happy; that not one of us would exchange the neighborly bliss of living on Main Street for the heathen gaudiness of New York or Paris or Stockholm. But in Mr. Garland's *Main-Travelled Roads* I discovered that there was one man who believed that Midwestern peasants were sometimes bewildered and hungry and vile—and heroic. And, given this vision, I was released; I could write of life as living life."

Ionic-pillared bank building in Sauk Center, Minn., Lewis's "Gopher Prairie," is now a beauty parlor.

Lewis felt that the American small town might have been ignored had it remained passive, but "it had become a force seeking to dominate the earth," a place of "small busy men . . . viewing themselves men of the world but keeping themselves men of the cash-register and the comic film, who make the town a sterile oligarchy . . . attempting to subject the entire country to the domination of the fundamentalists, prohibitionists, hundred per cent Americans and go-getters."

So Lewis emerged as recorder of the American middle class in the years between the two great wars. His people feel there is something wrong but they haven't the strength to rise above Main Street and they finally escape or give in. Or, like Carol Kennicott, they learn to dramatize themselves to survive in a world they can't face and can't hope to change.

Satirist in the guise of a realist, Lewis loved to undress the respectable Babbitts, Gantrys, and Dodsworths who were molding others into members of a "mighty herd that roamed the American plains." His occasional glimpses of a land where the artist or scientist is supreme are quickly effaced by his worlds of material progress, with the realtor and broker in charge.

In all the town not one building save the Ionic bank which gave pleasure to Carol's eyes; not a dozen buildings which suggested that, in the fifty years of Gopher Prairie's existence, the citizens had realized that it was either desirable or possible to make this, their common home, amusing or attractive.

—MAIN STREET

Once up in arms against Lewis, Sauk Center's Main Street is today proud of its native son.

Main Street with its two-story brick shops, its story-and-a-half wooden residences, its muddy expanse from concrete walk to walk, its huddle of Fords and lumber-wagons, was too small to absorb her. The broad, straight, unenticing gashes of the streets let in the grasping prairie on every side. She realized the vastness and the emptiness of the land.

—MAIN STREET

All I could see from where I stood
Was three long mountains and a wood;
I turned and looked the other way,
And saw three islands in a bay.
So with my eyes I traced the line
Of the horizon, thin and fine,
Straight around till I was come
Back to where I'd started from . . .

—RENASCENCE

Wind-lashed Matinicus lies off Penobscot Bay.

Hearing your words, and not a word among them
Tuned to my liking, on a salty day
When inland woods were pushed by winds that
flung them
Hissing to leeward like a ton of spray,
I thought how off Matinicus the tide
Came pounding in, came running through the Gut,
While from the Rock the warning whistle cried,
And children whimpered, and the doors blew
shut; . . .

—SONNET XXXVI

EDNA ST. VINCENT MILLAY

Love of the sea, the islands, and the Maine coast where she grew up and spent her latter summers fills the poetry of Edna St. Vincent Millay. It speaks out of the opening lines of her first major published work, the long poem *Renascence*, written in 1912 before she went to college. It runs through her impersonal songs of New England, and the memorable sonnet on the women of sea-born Matinicus Island.

"Vincent" had written since childhood, encouraged by her mother, and early verses appeared in the children's magazine *St. Nicholas*. Her first collection appeared shortly after she left Vassar. Of *Renascence*, Harriet Monroe wrote: "One would have to go back a long way in literary history to find a young lyric poet singing so freely and musically in such a big world."

Greenwich Village in its bohemian heyday attracted young Edna Millay and she became its chief spokesman in the "flaming youth," free-love, post-war rebellion against Victorian convention. Though in retrospect it has been suggested that this "burning the candle at both ends" phase, this making light of all emotion to the point of flippancy, was not Millay at her deepest, she nevertheless in that vein won a Pulitzer award for *The Harp Weavers*, and the Village sophisticate continued to crop up in her later work.

Edna St. Vincent Millay saw these "islands in a bay" near her Rockland, Maine, home.

. . . The sea howl
And the sea yelp, are different voices
Often together heard: the whine in the rigging,
The menace and caress of wave that breaks on water,
The distant rote in the granite teeth,
And the wailing warning from the approaching headland
Are all sea voices, and the heaving groaner
Rounded homewards, and the seagull:
And under the oppression of the silent fog
The tolling bell . . .

—THE DRY SALVAGES

T. S. ELIOT

A native Midwesterner now a British resident and subject, Thomas Stearns Eliot reflects his kinship with New England in his poetic imagery and his preoccupation with salvation. This is not surprising, for besides a celebrated New England ancestry and Harvard education he can count many summers spent at East Gloucester, Massachusetts, where he developed a love for the sea, expert ability as a sailor, and a familiarity with the rocky coasts of Cape Ann.

As he explains in an introductory note to *The Dry Salvages* (one of his later metaphysical poems published as part of *Four Quartets*), their name derives from the thin line of rocks just off the northeast coast of Cape Ann, presumably once *trois sauvages*, or three Indians. "Salvages" is pronounced to rhyme with "assuages." Like the other poems in the volume, *The Dry Salvages* is concerned with the meanings of experience and spiritual reality.

The early Eliot is remembered as one of the leading Anglo-American poets and one who first brought the invigorating ideas and forms of the French Symbolists to American and English literature. His scholarly *The Waste Land*, a poetic and intellectual milestone of the between-wars period, was a rebellion, popular in spite of its complexity and aristocratic tone of disillusion, against the aridity of a standardized modern civilization.

Eliot's more recent quest for tradition, which English critics choose to see as "typically American," has turned his outlook to the past. He became, as he himself once remarked, "an Anglo-Catholic in religion, a classicist in literature, and a royalist in politics."

On a moonless night the blinking lights of Cape Ann

and the Dry Salvages offshore illuminate the Atlantic at Rockport, Mass. Light line on horizon is passing ship.

Robinson Jeffers

On the outskirts of Carmel, where the Pacific pounds the sharp rocks, stands Tor House with its Hawk Tower. A screen of dark Australian pine and cypress shields it on three sides, and unambiguous no-trespassing signs warn any would-be intruders away from the fourth.

It took Robinson Jeffers four or five years to build this uninviting tower out of the rocks he gathered one by one from the sea, and he couldn't have constructed a retreat more in keeping with his dour literary personality.

Jeffers is a shy, introverted man who has lived in Carmel since 1914. Revolted by humanity, he has turned toward nature, a somber nature he knows from his rocky coasts. His powerful narratives, bearing on the emotional and sexual aberrations of coast ranch folk, play against a rich backdrop: cañons, river valleys, the lighthouses of Points Lobos and Sur, the flowers and birds of the region —gulls, eagles, and condors—the dark rocks, the "black cypress depths of ocean," and the granite mountains.

Profoundly affected by World War I and by his reading of nineteenth-century philosophy and twentieth-century psychology, Jeffers concludes that life today is horrible and incestuous, and civilization a sickness that the world could profitably do without. His poetry is an example of the lengths to which intellectual and emotional isolation can drive a sensitive person.

Jeffers's grandson plays in the yard of Tor House built by the poet's hands in 1924.

Tor House stands by the sea at Carmel, Calif.

Look for foundations of sea-worn granite, my fingers had the art
To make stone love stone, you will find some remnant.
But if you should look in your idleness after ten thousand years:
It is the granite knoll on the granite
And lava tongue in the midst of the bay, by the mouth of the Carmel
River-valley, these four will remain
In the change of names. . . .

—TOR HOUSE

Theodore Dreiser

After Theodore Dreiser had devoted considerable thought and several novels to the theme of the "survival of the fittest"—studies of American business magnates—he came to believe that the struggle of the unfit, the semiconscious, and the helpless against the forces that shaped their destinies was more typical of American life than was the occasional success of a genius or a tycoon.

In particular, his interest turned toward one problem: the crime arising from social or financial ambition. Several criminal cases of this nature had come to his attention over the years, but the one he eventually settled on as the basis for *An American Tragedy* was that of Chester Gillette of Cortland, N. Y., condemned in 1906 for the murder of Grace Brown, a factory worker from Otselic. To familiarize himself further with his subject he visited the Sing Sing death cells, interviewed a condemned murderer, and discussed with Dr. A. A. Brill, a leading psychiatrist, the psychology of murder.

The more Dreiser studied the case of Gillette—who became "Clyde Griffiths" in his tale—the more strongly he was convinced that the man had not been a "killer" but the victim of a characteristic American dream: in trying to better his lot he had done what he thought the approved thing. Ironically, he murdered to gain respectability in a society whose acceptance he desperately sought, and fell prey to the very standards to which he had tried to conform.

In other respects, too, Dreiser tried to trace "American" aspects of the case. His biographer, F. O. Matthiessen, noted that Clyde was drawn against a family background of ignorance and illusory moralism. During the trial, his guilt or innocence was submerged in a political fight between Republican prosecution and Democratic defense. Dreiser rejected both morality and traditional notions of the free individual, and in so doing eliminated the bases for a classic tragedy. In their stead he put the tragedy of man's struggle with overwhelming forces that he can neither control nor escape.

The censorship of *An American Tragedy* when it appeared in 1925 was no novelty to Dreiser, whose *Sister Carrie* and *The Genius* had been similarly handled in 1900 and 1915. Hailed as "the greatest American novel of our generation," the book brought Dreiser his first popularity and financial success.

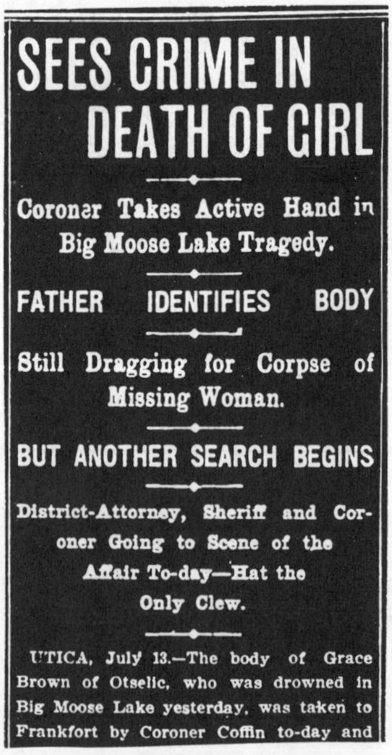

SEES CRIME IN DEATH OF GIRL

Coronar Takes Active Hand in Big Moose Lake Tragedy.

FATHER IDENTIFIES BODY

Still Dragging for Corpse of Missing Woman.

BUT ANOTHER SEARCH BEGINS

District-Attorney, Sheriff and Coroner Going to Scene of the Affair To-day—Hat the Only Clew.

UTICA, July 13.—The body of Grace Brown of Otselic, who was drowned in Big Moose Lake yesterday, was taken to Frankfort by Coroner Coffin to-day and

Story of the drowning of Grace Brown by Chester Gillette was the basis for Theodore Dreiser's novel.

And as they glided into this, this still dark water seemed to grip Clyde as nothing here or anywhere before this ever had. . . . Truly, it seemed to mock him—this strangeness—this dark pool, surrounded on all sides . . . like a huge, black pearl cast by some mighty hand, in anger possibly, in sport or phantasy maybe, into the bosom of this valley of dark, green plush—and which seemed bottomless as he gazed into it.

And yet, what did it all suggest so strongly? Death! Death! . . .

—AN AMERICAN TRAGEDY

Big Moose Lake, in the Adirondacks, was the scene of *An American Tragedy*.

A smoke-veiled Chicago skyline shows off its industrial might. Stockyard hogpens stand in the foreground.

Hog Butcher for the World,
Tool Maker, Stacker of Wheat,
Player with Railroads and the
Nation's Freight Handler;
Stormy, husky, brawling,
City of the Big Shoulders: . . .

—CHICAGO

CARL SANDBURG

Before Carl Sandburg became a poet he had been a dishwasher, door-to-door salesman, harvest hand, movie reviewer, bell ringer, janitor, soldier, and reporter, and he had tramped all over America, particularly the West. Son of a Swedish workman, he knew American workmen of all origins and when he became a poet he wanted to be their poet.

In 1914 *Poetry* printed some of his work while he was a Chicago newspaper reporter, and his *Chicago* won him a $200 prize. Critics saw a strong new voice, a disregard for poetic convention, a radical choice of subject, a slangy manner, and a lusty independence. Deeply influenced by Whitman, Sandburg was first to speak for the tough, machine-bred Midwestern city people, for the sun-drenched farmers of the Midwestern plains, and for the whole of modern America. Known first as a poet, he thinks of himself primarily as an "American folk-song recitalist" and has gained additional stature with his monumental Lincoln biography.

West of town lie many of the waterways and railroads of the "Nation's Freight Handler."

Horseshoe pitching is still a favorite among oldsters of St. Petersburg's Sunshine Pleasure Club.

Well, Mother and I put in a great day watching the pitchers and she wanted I should get in the game, but I told her I was all out of practice and would make a fool of myself, though I seen several men pitching who I guess I could take their measure without no practice.

—THE GOLDEN HONEYMOON

Ring Lardner

During the "roaring twenties" all America was off on a spree, Florida boomed as a national playground, and Ringgold W. Lardner, a Midwestern sports writer already established as a ranking humorist, became the self-styled and hilarious historian of Florida-bound Mr. and Mrs. America, mixing among the "high polloi" of swanky Palm Beach.

Lardner's deft handling of his naïvely fatheaded, stingy bush-leaguer in *You Know Me Al* started a healthy trend of cynicism in sports reporting, and *Champion* decisively "kayoed" any further adulation of our sports idols as paragons of modesty and virtue. When Lardner turned his distaste for hot air in sports to an obsession with phoniness everywhere, small-town boorishness (*Haircut*), as well as suburban hypocrisy (*The Love Nest*), were fair game for his vitriolic, slangy, almost always funny, pen. Americans from Niles, Michigan, to Miami, Florida, could understand his language. Less understood, though better comprehended since his death in 1933, was the laugh-obscured bitterness, the despair for a Babbitt-ridden human race. Future generations, looking back on Lardner with delight, may see, as William Bolitho did, the "greatest and sincerest pessimist America has produced."

Ponce de Leon still graces St. Augutine.

The hotel's named after the fella that built it. He come from Spain and they say he was huntin' for some water that if he'd drunk it he'd feel young. I don't see myself how you could expect to feel young on water. But, anyway, he'd heard that this here kind o' water could be found in St. Augustine, and when he couldn't find it he went into the hotel business and got even with the United States by chargin' five dollars a day and up for a room.

—GULLIBLE'S TRAVELS

. . . Menéndez called his landing place St. Augustine.

The Mass of Our Lady was then celebrated, so the tale says—upon Ocean Street, but a little distance to the east of where San Marco Avenue develops into Dixie Highway and enters a gaunt grove of billboards commemorative, for interminable miles, of competitive dealers in pecans. Upon this same plot of ground just south of Ocean Street was erected, later, and still stands, the Chapel of Nuestra Señora de la Léche y Buen Parto. Such was the beginning of our civilization, with the founding of the first Christian city in the United States of America.

—THE FIRST GENTLEMAN OF AMERICA

JAMES BRANCH CABELL

Even the intrepid Pedro Menéndez de Avilés, habituated to strange sights during his adventurous career in the service of Spain, would gape if he could see what the twentieth century has done to ancient St. Augustine, founded by him in 1565 as the first colonial city on the American continent. All trace of his settlement has disappeared, and in its place have risen "shrines" and pseudo-historical relics, the brain children of the Florida boom which James Branch Cabell lampoons in *The First Gentleman of America*, his satire on our early history.

While most American writers of the early twentieth century were breaking the romantic stranglehold by varying degrees of realism, Cabell, that deft "épateur of the bourgeoisie," turned in the opposite direction and spoofed American society allegorically by a fanciful return to the Middle Ages. A Virginian of old family, he steeped himself in history, genealogy, and the chivalric codes of old. Reality to him was convention; romance, the highest art, with its culmination the Cabell novels about the mythical "Manuel of Poictesme." One of these, *Jurgen*, created a literary furor in 1919 when an unsuccessful attempt was made to censor it.

Cabell was the supreme escapist of his day. Though he was extravagantly praised at the time, the responsive chord he struck among postwar sophisticates is today somewhat muted.

Billboards line Dixie Highway at St. Augustine, Fla.

La Leche Shrine
OPEN 8-5
513
Fountain of Youth
One Block
SERVICE
STANDARD OIL
CHEVROLET
SHELL
U.S. TIRES
USED
Welcome to
La Leche Shrine

Towers of Manhattan light up in midwinter dusk.

Dusk gently smooths crispangled streets. Dark presses tight the steaming asphalt city. . . . Under the rolling heavier pressure windows blurt light. Night crushes bright milk out of arclights, squeezes the sullen blocks until they drop red, yellow, green into streets resounding with feet. All the asphalt oozes light. . . .

—MANHATTAN TRANSFER

John Dos Passos

In *Manhattan Transfer,* John Dos Passos used the new device of the "collectivistic novel" to paint the complex life of a metropolis. Writing in the naturalist tradition, with a stern belief that "ugliness must be shown, even if it hurts," he attempted a history of New York from 1890 to 1925, showing in successive glimpses the lives of a wide variety of people representing different metropolitan strata. The result was a kaleidoscopic crisscross of rising and falling destinies, each revealed for a breathless moment but never fully developed. It makes for a dazzling show, but he leaves no doubt that with all the complex city organization—milk delivery, fire department, traffic control—the city's inhabitants live side by side without basic relations or feelings, in a world of social and moral chaos.

A sensitive idealist, deeply affected by World War I, Dos Passos first touched on his favorite thesis of "man versus society" (with society generally the winner) in *Three Soldiers,* an early war-deflating work, and carried it through to his monumental trilogy, *U. S. A.*

Lower New York looms from the Bay to dawn ferrygoers.

Across the zinc water the tall walls, the birchlike cluster of downtown buildings shimmered up the rosy morning like a sound of horns through a chocolatebrown haze. As the boat drew near the buildings densened to a granite mountain split with knifecut canyons.

—MANHATTAN TRANSFER

John Brown's "fort," once on grassy embankment (right) in Harpers Ferry, W. Va., has since been moved.

STEPHEN VINCENT BENÉT

They reached the Maryland Bridge of Harper's
Ferry
That Sunday night. There were twenty-two in all,
Nineteen were under thirty, three not twenty-one,
Kagi, the self-taught scholar, quiet and cool,
Stevens, the cashiered soldier, Puritan-fathered,
A singing giant, gunpowder-tempered and
rash. . . .

—JOHN BROWN'S BODY

John Brown, Thoreau once said, was the kind of man "it takes ages to make and ages to understand." Surely this Old Testament figure of wrath, whose conscience made him stand off the U. S. Army at Harpers Ferry in the cause of antislavery, has aroused America's poetic imagination. Stephen Vincent Benét, a poet "in love with American names," loved also its ballads and folk heroes. Into *John Brown's Body*, his major narrative and a Pulitzer prize winner in 1929, he put all this emotion plus an exhaustive knowledge of the period. It is as a folk-balladist that Benét, who came of a poetic family, will be remembered. Even his folk tales in the Irving tradition, such as the delightful *Devil and Daniel Webster*, are really "prose" in name only.

The slender span of Brooklyn Bridge ties lower New York to Long Island.

HART CRANE

TO BROOKLYN BRIDGE

And Thee, across the harbor, silver-paced
As though the sun took step of thee, yet left
Some motion ever unspent in thy stride,—
Implicitly thy freedom staying thee!

—THE BRIDGE

Hart Crane selected Brooklyn Bridge as "the most beautiful artifact in North America" when he was on the lookout for a poetic symbol worthy of the fundamental spirit of this country and its people. Strongly influenced by Whitman, he saw the bridge as a link joining past to present, present to future, life to death, nonbeing to birth, Old World to New.

Crane was a tragic figure among contemporary writers. Torn between his separated parents, dominated by a well-intentioned father determined to "shake the poetic nonsense" out of him, later subsidized by a rich patron, he tottered into a confused morass of alcoholism, undiscipline, and homosexuality whose only exit was the suicide he committed in 1932. His legacy, *The Bridge* and *White Buildings*, though hard to read, was nonetheless promise of a genius that was never fulfilled.

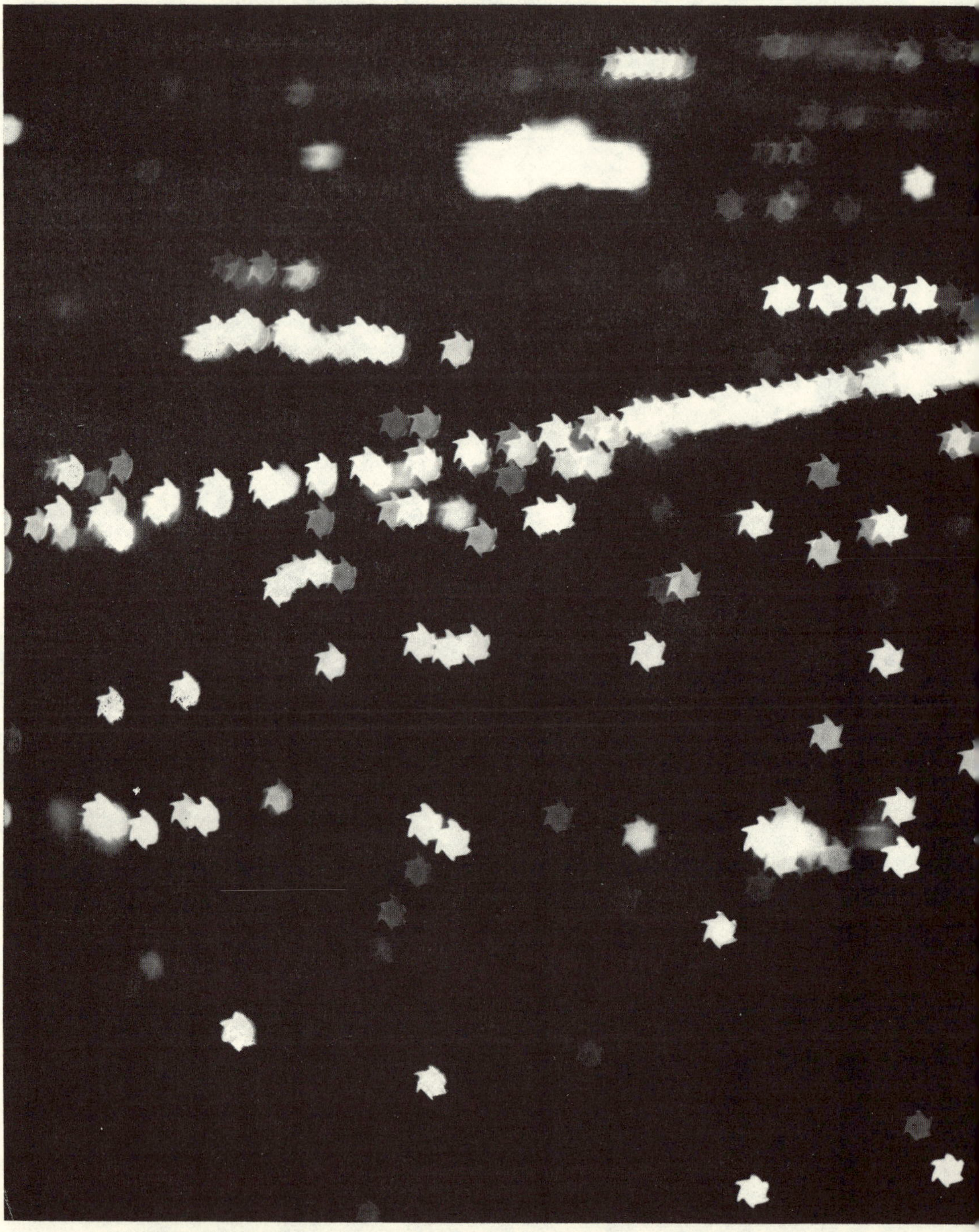

From on high the lights of star-laden Hollywood glistened to Monroe Stahr, Fitzgerald's "Last Tycoon."

The motors were off, and all our five senses began to readjust themselves for landing . . . this was where Stahr had come to earth after that extraordinary illuminating flight where he saw which way we were going, and how we looked doing it, and how much of it mattered . . . in a "long shot" he saw a new way of measuring our jerky hopes and graceful rogueries and awkward sorrows and . . . he came here from choice to be with us to the end. Like the plane coming down into the Glendale airport, into the warm darkness.

—THE LAST TYCOON

F. SCOTT FITZGERALD

More than any other writer of the twenties, Francis Scott Fitzgerald spoke for the flippant, hard-boiled, disillusioned young generation that left a trail of empty bottles and tired bodies on its mad escapade through the roaring decade.

He was a Midwesterner of Irish and Southern origin, and though not of their class he became the chronicler and desperate emulator of the rich, blond scions of old Eastern families whose lives moved between Long Island and the Riviera. After *This Side of Paradise*, his identification in the public mind with "flaming youth" was complete. Sadly, the eternal youth never quite grew up, though his generation did. Financial and personal problems beset him, and few of his large following knew that he had escaped to the last bit of never-never land in America, Hollywood.

From the Hollywood period, nevertheless, came *The Last Tycoon*, his last and most mature novel. In it the author is again dealing with a vital, if flamboyant, slice of life, but this time his hero is neither a bootlegger nor a socialite, but a self-made mogul of a vitally important American industry. In film producer Monroe Stahr, Fitzgerald saw the end of the Jazz Age, "that escape into a lavish, romantic past that perhaps will not come again in our time." His sudden death in 1940 left *The Last Tycoon* only a fragment, but one that showed what may have been a different, more mature Fitzgerald developing.

Oxford, Miss., is an important Faulkner locale.

. . . We watched Judge Dukinfield as he went daily between his home and his office in the courthouse yard. Deliberate and unhurried he moved—a widower of sixty and more, portly, white-headed, with an erect and dignified carriage which the Negroes called 'rear-backted.'

—SMOKE

William Faulkner

The world of William Faulkner, the imaginary Yoknapatawpha County, is the northern Mississippi country lying between the pine-clad sandhills and the black earth lowlands of the river valley. "Jefferson," its capital, is a composite of many small towns of the area—New Albany, where the novelist was born, Holly Springs, or Ripley. It is certainly also Oxford, Faulkner's present home.

Son of one of the old families that opened up and owned the land in this area, Faulkner, like so many contemporary writers, fought in World War I and came out of it with blighted illusions. Unlike them, he did not repair to the Left Bank, but stayed at home to contemplate his own fate and that of the South. The result has been a series of novels full of intensity and violence, of frequent obscure overwriting, but just as frequent brilliant narration. He

It took him two years, he and his crew of imported slaves. . . . But he was a good architect; Quentin knew the house, twelve miles from Jefferson, in its grove of cedar and oak. . . . And not only an architect . . . but an artist, since only an artist could have borne those two years in order to build a house which he doubtless not only expected but firmly intended never to see again.

—ABSALOM, ABSALOM!

The old Shipp Place, unpainted and falling apart, stands on a forgotten stage road south of Oxford.

"Sutpen's" country store could have been this one on the main highway south of Oxford.

The "dogtrot" cabin with its open areaway in the middle is a home for many Faulkner characters.

. . . It was in the rear of the little store which Sutpen managed to set up on the highroad . . . where . . . he dispensed kerosene and staple foodstuffs and stale gaudy candy and cheap beads and ribbons to Negroes or poor whites . . . who came afoot or on gaunt mules to haggle tediously for dimes and quarters with a man who at one time could gallop . . . ten miles across his own fertile land and who had led troops gallantly in battle. . . .

—THE UNVANQUISHED

William Faulkner

is the first American writer since 1938 to receive the Nobel prize.

Throughout his stories of events in the lives of Southerners—aristocrats, poor whites, Indians, Negroes—runs, as a symbolic undercurrent, the legend of the South: how an order was established by the planters on Indian land, how slavery grew to be the curse of this order and brought on the Civil War, how a new class arose among the landless whites to challenge the rule of the old planters. At this juncture Faulkner yearns in despair for a South of the past, watching in hatred this new "Snopes" class, again cursed by having turned "servants of the North," destroying a country that old Southerners would preserve but in their weakness cannot.

In the midst of this conflict Faulkner reveals two of his major obsessions. Haunted by the idea of miscegenation, he has come to look upon both the emancipated Negro and the modern Southern woman as its chief perpetrators and the source of the South's destruction. An ambivalent thread, his love for the land and his fear of its devastation, runs through his voluminous work. As one critic pointed out, his is a strange combination of civilization and savagery—like one of his colonial mansions in a cypress swamp.

It was a big, squarish frame house that had once been white, decorated with cupolas and spires and scrolled balconies in the heavily lightsome style of the seventies, set on what had once been our most select street. But garages and cotton gins had encroached and obliterated even the august names of that neighborhood; only Miss Emily's house was left, lifting its stubborn and coquettish decay above the cotton wagons and the gasoline pumps—an eyesore among eyesores.

—A ROSE FOR EMILY

White frame house in Holly Springs, Miss., recalls Faulkner's "Emily."

. . . Nick pulled the boat high up the beach. . . . In back of them was the close second-growth timber of the point and in front was the bay with the mouth of Hortons Creek. It was not quite dark. The firelight went as far as the water. . . .

—THE END OF SOMETHING

ERNEST HEMINGWAY

Though Ernest Hemingway was born and intermittently educated in Oak Park, Ill., he regarded as his real home the woody tip of northern Michigan where he spent his summers. Memories of the woods where he hunted dot the early stories that appeared under the title *In Our Time*. Some of his landmarks, like the old lumber mill at Horton Bay, have gone, but the general store with its "high false front" is still around, and the sandy road still drops down to the bay where tall pines darken the water.

When *In Our Time* appearea, critics at first remarked the contrast between its "idyllic" Michigan stories and the grim war episodes; but a closer reading showed even in the childhood memoirs of outdoor life, fishing, swimming, an early Hemingwayan preoccupation with brutality and death, the major themes of all his later work. He was one of the youngest of the "lost generation" expatriates, and wrote after intimate contact with a war in which he had been not only severly wounded but badly disillu-

Horton Bay (right) and its general store in northern Michigan are much as Hemingway saw them.

sioned—life was full of violence, short pleasures, constant danger, and nothing more.

When after ten years of "war, blood, isolation, and death"—a decade which produced *The Sun Also Rises* and *A Farewell to Arms*—the author moved to Key West and wrote *To Have and Have Not,* critics saw in it a new and more affirmative "Papa" Hemingway, whose tough Harry Morgan realized gropingly at his death that "no man alone ain't got no bloody chance." Many feel that *For Whom the Bell Tolls* marked a still further attempt toward a more positive philosophy.

From Gertrude Stein he learned to use words that convey an emotion sharply and essentially; and in content as well as in form there is no doubt that Hemingway has exerted a preponderant influence on present-day writing in general and on the short story in particular.

Hemingway's Harry Morgan moored borrowed boat at foot of Porter Dock in Key West.

"I've got gas at the house in the tank," he told Bee-lips. . . .

"They wanted you to be right at the Porter Dock."

"How can I lay there with this boat?"

"You can't. But I don't think they'll want to do any car driving."

—TO HAVE AND HAVE NOT

BURYING GROUND BY THE TIES

. . . It was we laid the steel on this land from ocean
to ocean:
It was we (if you know) put the U. P. through the
passes

Bringing her down into Laramie full load
Eighteen mile on the granite anticlinal
Forty-three foot to the mile and the grade holding:

. . . Who would do it but we and the Irishmen
bossing us?
It was all foreign-born men there were in this coun-
try;
It was Scotsmen Englishmen Chinese Squareheads
Austrians . . .

Ayee! but there's weight to the earth under it:
Not for this did we come out—to be lying here
Nameless under the ties in the clay cuts: . . .

—FRESCOES FOR MR. ROCKEFELLER'S CITY

Forgotten graves lie near the Union Pacific Railway tracks leading down-grade into Laramie, Wyoming.

ARCHIBALD MACLEISH

One of the young men who, after Hotchkiss, Yale, and Harvard, had fought in the Great War and experienced the Grand Illusion, Archibald MacLeish identified himself with the "lost generation" exiles who preferred Paris to the crass boom years of America. Coming under the influence of Ezra Pound and T. S. Eliot, he had written poetry whose titles, *Tower of Ivory* and *The Hamlet of A. MacLeish* suggest his introspection and anxiety over "Man's uncertain place in the unknown."

After five years abroad, he decided in 1928 that his roots were, after all, in America, a country he had regarded as "neither a land nor a race." *Frescoes for Mr. Rockefeller's City* was a result of this rediscovery. In it, and in *New Found Land* and *Conquistador* he turned to broad historical American themes and a scrutiny of the people who made up the land. With his patrician background he had some difficulty in ridding himself of certain stereotypes about this people, but his poetry now had some of the air of the wide American spaces and caught a spirit of those who worked its soil. He moved still further from the ivory tower in later experiments with (to him) newer media of theater, ballet, and radio, and was made Librarian of Congress and later head of wartime propaganda.

PUZZLED

Here on the edge of hell
Stands Harlem—
Remembering the old lies,
The old kicks in the back,
The old, Be patient,
They told us before.

Sure, we remember.
Now, when the man at the corner store
Says sugar's gone up another two cents,
And bread one,
And there's a new tax on cigarettes—
We remember the job we never had,
Never could get,
And can't have now
Because we're colored.

So we stand here
On the edge of hell
In Harlem
And look out on the world
And wonder
What we're gonna do
In the face of
What we remember.

—ONE-WAY TICKET

Langston Hughes

Langston Hughes first attracted professional attention to himself as a poet (he had had poems published in his school paper in Cleveland) when he laid a sheaf of poems next to Vachel Lindsay's dinner plate at the Wardman Park Hotel in Washington. Hughes was working as a busboy, and Lindsay, there for one of his recitals, later read the young man's poems with his own.

Hughes had been raised in his native Joplin, Mo., by a grandmother who was the last surviving widow of John Brown's raiding party. He had traveled the Southwest, Midwest, and Mexico, had been to the West Coast of Africa as a seaman, cooked in a Montmartre night club, visited Italy, and finally "painted" his way back to America as a sailor assigned to keep his ship whitewashed.

Weary Blues, his first collection, appeared a year after his return. Since then he has written short stories, film scripts, a Broadway success (*Mulatto*), and children's books, covered the Spanish Civil War as the only American Negro correspondent, and edited an anthology of Negro poetry.

Langston Hughes was in his early work preoccupied with Harlem life, jazz rhythms, the fate of Negroes, and a longing for the warmth and beauty he had found in the tropical lands he had visited. His concern with broader social issues confronting Negroes and whites, and all racial minorities, was seen to grow in *Scottsboro Limited, Four Poems and a Play in Verse*, and *The Ways of White Folks*. His deceptively dumb-wise Harlem creation, "Simple," is on his way to becoming a folk legend. Hughes's verse has been translated into German, French, Yiddish, Spanish, Russian, and Czech.

Two from Harlem stand on the edge of their teeming hell.

From high on Beaucatcher Mountain, Thomas Wolfe looked down on his "Altamont," Asheville, N. C.

. . . The town was thrown up on the plateau like an encampment. There was nothing below him that could resist time. There was no idea. Below him, in a cup, he felt that all life was held: he saw it as might one of the old schoolmen writing in monkish Latin a Theatre of Human Life; or like Peter Breughel, in one of his swarming pictures. It seemed to him suddenly that he had not come up on the hill from the town, but that he had come out of the wilderness like a beast, and was staring now with steady beast-eye at this little huddle of wood and mortar which the wilderness must one day repossess, devour, cover over.

—LOOK HOMEWARD, ANGEL

"Dixieland," his mother's boardinghouse, was really called "My Old Kentucky Home."

Thomas Wolfe

Anyone who has read at least one of Thomas Wolfe's sprawling novels knows all about "Altamont" or "Libya Hill"—it is always Wolfe's home town of Asheville, nestling high up in the smoky blue mountains of North Carolina.

When *Look Homeward, Angel* first came out "there was hell to pay in Asheville." Surprised by the hostile reception, Wolfe recalled in his *Story of a Novel* how "for months the town seethed with a fury of resentment," how the book was denounced from the pulpit by leading ministers, how it was the chief topic of acrimonious chatter on street corners ···omen's clubs and teas. Among the most riled were his mother's family, but she herself said she would stand by the book as long as it was a success, even if it did call the family names and she couldn't quite grasp its meaning.

Over the years the town lost its grudge, as "Gopher Prairie" did in Sinclair Lewis's case. A "Wolfe Memorial" bought "Dixieland" after Mrs. Wolfe died and is preserving it just as it was in the days of this mercurial family. Wolfe *aficionados* will be transported back into the novels and recognize rooms, objects, almost the smell, that affected young "Eugene" so profoundly.

Though he wrote prodigiously, filling four fat

In this bed, where all Wolfe children were born, little Tom sometimes slept with older brother Ben.

volumes, one theme prevailed: the quest for a meaning of life as Wolfe saw it in America. He hoped that by re-creating first his childhood, then his youth, he could find an answer. With the frenzied energy and naïve egotism of a small-town boy who feels he's facing the world alone, Wolfe set out on his hegira. During it he exposed, in a prose often soaring to magnificent poetic heights, areas of American life untapped by any other writer.

Reared in an emotion-starved, penny-grabbing home, he pursued a life that was richer and that he knew, from his voracious reading, existed. His posthumous, and post-depression, *You Can't Go Home Again* has the beginnings of a pattern emerging from the chaos, a turning from the terrifying aloneness at last to a sense of oneness with humanity.

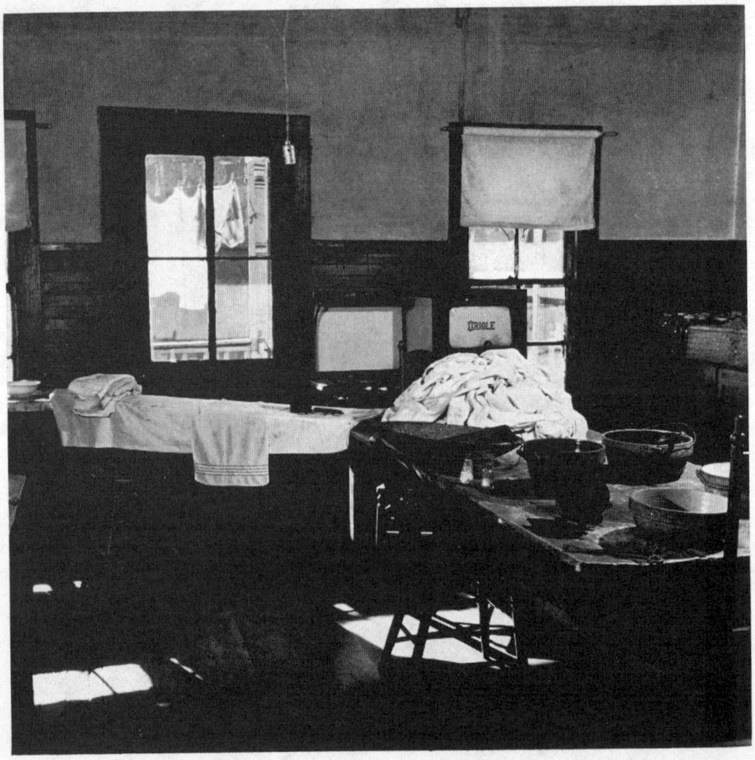

The kitchen where Mrs. Wolfe reigned is as she left it, with a pile of unironed wash.

An angel of Italian marble that once stood outside "Gant's" shop adorns Hendersonville, N. C., grave.

And the angels on Gant's porch were frozen in hard marble silence, and at a distance life awoke. . . .

Yet, as he stood for the last time by the angels of his father's porch, it seemed as if the Square already were far and lost . . . he was like a man who stands upon a hill above the town he has left, yet does not say "The town is near," but turns his eyes upon the distant soaring ranges.

—LOOK HOMEWARD, ANGEL

"McGinty" admired bridges over Chicago River.

. . . Slowly, exactly, the bridge arms lifted, till its span pointed to the sky, and the approaching boat came between them. . . .

Why, that bridge opening that way was like a miracle, like God was doing it. It was figures worked out, that's what it was, figures like the figures he liked to work out at night. That bridge pointing to the sky was figures worked out neat, on clean white sheets of paper, with no mistakes, and no erasures. . . .

—GAS-HOUSE MCGINTY

JAMES T. FARRELL

James T. Farrell wrote the trilogy *Studs Lonigan*, he said, to "drive this neighborhood and all its memories out of my consciousness." Like Studs, he was the child of an Irish-American family on Chicago's tough South Side, where poolrooms, smutty jokes, promiscuity, liquor, and fighting were his education, and Farrell saw his friends sink slowly into a slough of family bickering, piety, ill-health, and insecurity. He himself escaped by way of the "atheist" University of Chicago.

The *Studs Lonigan* series, on which his reputation is largely based, is the study of an average American city boy growing up in the early part of this century affected and infected by his environment. This is the world of the ward politician and the parish school, a world where man's only known creations were foul language and the sensational movie and his chief intellectual stimulants liquor and sex. In *Gas-House McGinty*, Farrell turned to the endeavors of a man to keep up his self-esteem in the face of the petty rivalries and frustrations of life in a vast transcontinental express company.

A young writer of the thirties whose viewpoint differed radically from that of the preceding "lost generation," Farrell is noteworthy for a frank, carefully detailed, naturalistic, and above all objective presentation of a social and psychological milieu which invites the reader to draw his own conclusions. His books were and still are important milestones of fiction of the thirties.

"58th and Prairie," in South Chicago, was Studs Lonigan's (and Farrell's) domain.

Georgia shacks and unkempt yards are reminiscent of Erskine Caldwell's "Lesters" in *Tobacco Road.*

. . . The stones had been laid one on top of the other, the beams spiked, and the house nailed together. The ease and simplicity with which it had been built was now evident. The centre of the building sagged between the sills; the front porch had sagged loose from the house, and was now a foot or more lower than it originally was. . . . Most of the shingles had rotted. . . . The house had never been painted.

—TOBACCO ROAD

Erskine Caldwell

By 1930 the trend of "lost" souls pondering the hopelessness of their lives in Parisian bistros had about run its course, and writers were beginning to wonder what was becoming of America since the boom, the crash of '29, and the subsequent depression. Writing during the New Deal years consisted largely in a general stocktaking of how our economic and social traditions had fared.

One of the new young writers taking stock was Erskine Caldwell, a minister's son from eastern Georgia whose firsthand knowledge of his own province, plus a rare humor, resulted in *Tobacco Road.* In it the moral and social disintegration of his poor-white "Lesters" is equated with the disintegration of the land. In the vastly successful theatrical version of *Tobacco Road* is further highlighted poor Jeeter Lester's last-ditch devotion to that land—his single, if illusory, asset.

Century-old soil abuse, lack of education, absentee ownership, share-cropping, and finally depression had reduced the small Southern farmer to utter ruin, and—according to Caldwell's *Some American People*—hundreds were dying of starvation, others hid behind trees when strangers passed because they were naked, religious fanaticism was rampant, illiteracy the general rule, infant mortality soaring, venereal disease common, and incest as prevalent as marriage.

Though poverty and share-cropping persist, the extremes of "Tobacco Road" have disappeared today. Rural electrification, soil conservation, and war prosperity have changed the region. Houses have tin roofs in place of the Lesters' leaky shingles; and deep-freezes on rickety porches and "picture windows" are not rare sights. With it all, Caldwell's powers seem to have faded somewhat, though the current vast sale of his Georgia tales, in 25-cent reprint form, is testimony to his earlier literary skill.

Though rural poverty persists, many houses like this are no longer inhabited.

Highway 66 was the route of flight for the "Okies."

People in flight along 66. And the concrete road shone like a mirror under the sun, and in the distance the heat made it seem that there were pools of water in the road. . . .

—THE GRAPES OF WRATH

JOHN STEINBECK

When John Steinbeck's *The Grapes of Wrath* appeared, it was, in the words of one critic, "burned and banned, borrowed, smuggled, but above all, bought." While Erskine Caldwell was writing about a rural people too far gone to move off their worthless patches of land, Steinbeck presented the plight of the "Okies," migrant farmers of Oklahoma, Arkansas, Arizona, and Texas, whom decades of overcultivation, a corrupt land policy, drought, bank foreclosure, and finally depression had "dusted-out, tractored-out, or starved-out" of their small holdings. Through the "Joads" he told how these thousands, in patched-up jalopies, fled along Highway 66 to the promised land of California. There they were herded into packing-crate "Hoovervilles," picked fruit at below-subsistence wages, fought hopelessly with the giant farm-canning-railroad interests, and eventually—their self-respect all but gone—succumbed to starvation and disease. Today, the jalopies are gone, and whatever "Okies" are left are no longer a national but a local community problem, as is attested by the outlying slums of many a San Joaquin Valley town.

The Grapes of Wrath, a publishing bonanza and a prize-winning film, firmly established a writer whose versatility had already produced poetry, drama, historical romance, and psychological analysis. Born in California, educated as a marine biologist, Steinbeck tried hod carrying, house painting, caretaking, surveying, reporting, and fruit-picking before his writing began to pay off. His was a literary craftsmanship that, while concerning itself more with the personal dramas of his semiarticulate men and women than with the issues involved in their plight, happily coincided with the widespread concern of a nation still licking its wounds after its recent economic collapse.

At dusk on 66, mountain silhouettes mark the divide between dry Arizona and golden California.

The houses were left vacant on the land, and the land was vacant because of this. . . . The houses were vacant, and a vacant house falls quickly apart. . . .

On a night the wind loosened a shingle and flipped it to the ground. The next wind pried into the hole where the shingle had been, lifted off three, and the next, a dozen. . . .

—THE GRAPES OF WRATH

Migration left this empty farm near Sallisaw, Okla.

Curzon's Mill, Marquand family home, was the model for his *Wickford Point.*

JOHN P. MARQUAND

In those days at Wickford Point we were living on the comfortable tail-end of the Victorian era, but Wickford Point was so far removed from contemporary contacts that much of it was still early Victorian. Life still proceeded in the grooves worn by things which had happened before my parents were born.

—WICKFORD POINT

Whittier, in a little poem called *June on the Merrimac,* wrote: "And here are pictured Artichoke, And Curson's bowery mill; And Pleasant Valley smiles between the river and the Hill." Curzon's Mill, near Newburyport, Mass., gathering place of Marquand's fictional literati is the backdrop for John P. Marquand's *Wickford Point.* In it lived the "Brills," called "the most ghostly of decadent Puritans," twentieth-century descendants of eminent New England stock with nothing left but their pride of ancestry.

Through his series of satires on a dying New England, of which *The Late George Apley* is the first and most memorable, Marquand brought the postwar debunking school to New England. Before, he had been a prolific writer of magazine stories and creator of "Mr. Moto," and now he showed himself a masterly social satirist of his native heath, with a smooth and ironical style well adapted to the ultrasophisticated society he so deftly lampoons.

Richard Wright

After *Native Son* had become a best seller in 1940, Richard Wright explained in an article, *How Bigger Was Born,* that he had been storing impressions of its hero, Bigger Thomas, since his own childhood. There were many Biggers, from the ball-snatching one in Jackson, Miss., to the one driven insane by Jim Crow taboos. In Chicago he found the Biggers reacting almost more violently than in the South, dazzled by relatively greater hopes of real freedom.

Wright himself had undergone many of the trials that turned boys into Biggers. His aim in *Native Son* was to expose a social order, rather than any inherent trait, which had caused the frustration and rebellion of Negro youth in America. It was his anger that such a society had produced twelve million people who were "stunted, stripped and held captive within this nation" that led him to write it.

. . . The doorways were wider than those of any house in which he had ever lived. Some rich folks lived here once, he thought. Rich white folks. That was the way most houses on the South Side were, ornate, old, stinking; homes once of rich white people, now inhabited by Negroes or standing dark and empty. . . . He remembered that bombs had been thrown by whites into houses like these when Negroes had first moved into the South Side. . . .

—NATIVE SON

Former Chicago South Side mansions are now slums of Wright's "Native Son."

Margaret Mitchell

The thirties saw not only the rise of social and proletarian literature but also a sudden spurt in the popularity of the "historical novel," paced by Margaret Mitchell's *Gone With the Wind*, the American publishing phenomenon of all time. It sold 50,000 copies in one day, 6,000,000 all told, was translated into twenty-five languages and Braille, and grossed $38,000,000 as a Hollywood extravaganza.

Author of this giant was a petite Atlanta journalist steeped in Civil War history (she was ten before she learned that the South had lost), who felt that its Georgia phase had been neglected and began to write about it for her own amusement. The popularity of *G.W.T.W.* had twofold significance: it proved America's desire to read more about its past, and it reflected a universal urge to escape from current domestic and foreign crises into the glories of a more romantic period.

No "Tara" existed, but this Washington, Ga., home lies between Hollywood "Tara" and working farm of the book.

Only her feeling for Tara had not changed. She never came wearily home across the fields and saw the sprawling white house that her heart did not swell with love and the joy of homecoming. She never looked out of her window at green pastures and red fields and tall tangled swamp forest that a sense of beauty did not fill her. . . . Nowhere else in the world was there land like this.

—GONE WITH THE WIND

We were poor. We had no money. Our whole tribe was poverty-stricken. Every branch of the Garoghlanian family was living in the most amazing and comical poverty in the world. . . .

—MY NAME IS ARAM

Jeffrey Sarouhan plays in Fresno, Calif., back yards as his famous cousin did.

WILLIAM SAROYAN

Rows of small white houses still characterize that section of Fresno where most of the town's Armenian population has lived for decades and where young Bill Saroyan grew up among a host of cousins whom he still writes fondly about in his countless stories. An omnivorous reader since boyhood, he appeared first in an Armenian magazine. He worked at almost everything until the instant success of his first collection, *The Daring Young Man on the Flying Trapeze,* set him up as an author. His easy, tough-whimsical style has led some critics to call him the "genius" he unceasingly claims to be. Self-styled "bad boy" of American letters, he has been firmly established as a "character" at least. Theater, movies, and, recently, song writing have claimed him, and nobody would be surprised to see a new Saroyan grand opera, dictionary, or theory of relativity.

Jody's "flutter mill" was a "wheel" of palm fronds on a twig-axle, supported on two crotched sticks.

A spring as clear as well water bubbled up from nowhere in the sand. It was as though the banks cupped green leafy hands to hold it. There was a whirlpool where the water rose from the earth. Grains of sand boiled in it. . . . It excited Jody to watch the beginnings of the ocean . . .

—THE YEARLING

MARJORIE KINNAN RAWLINGS

At the bottom of a steep bluff in central Florida, vine-clad palms and mossy oaks form a silvery glen in whose center a white spring throws water into the air like a pigmy geyser. Fronds dip their spiky tips into the water and minnows dart among the moss-covered roots. This is where Jody, hero of *The Yearling*, came to wade in the velvet sand and build his flutter mill out of a palm leaf.

The Yearling, published in 1938, has become a minor American classic, as important for its contribution to our regional literature as it is appealing in its understanding of the engaging boy Jody. According to Marjorie Kinnan Rawlings, Jody was really two old men who regaled her with their fishing and hunting tales. To them she added her own knowledge of the Florida backwoods (she has lived on an orange grove near Cross Creek since 1928) and a warm appreciation of its people.

"Baxter's Island," really Pat's Island, near Silver Glen, Fla., had many water holes for game near by.

. . . It seemed to Jody that he moved in a dream between night and day, and when the sun rose, he would awaken. . . . A favorite water-hole of the game lay beyond. It was a clear deep pool and something about the water was to the taste of the creatures. It was protected as well with marsh on two sides, from which danger might be seen approaching, and forest on the other two, into which they might quickly retreat.

—THE YEARLING

In Silver Glen, Fla., lies the same bubbling spring that fascinated young Jody Baxter in *The Yearling*.

Oaks in Washington, Miss., on the Natchez Trace are the site of Aaron Burr's first treason trial.

Eudora Welty

Scattered over the United States are remnants of ancient roads, today forgotten, once the life arteries of sections of the nation. Some are foundations for modern superhighways, others have been effaced by time and technology. Of all, the Natchez Trace alone has preserved a good deal of its identity.

A prehistoric buffalo path, it was the chief route of the Choctaw and the Chickasaw. Later, it became the main road of colonization for Louisiana and the lands west of the Mississippi, the road for merchants and for bloody highwaymen, the road that sped the U. S. mails and the U. S. soldiers on their way to battle in New Orleans and Mexico. Men such as Sieur de Bienville, Henry Clay, Lorenzo Dow, Audubon, and Andrew Jackson rode over it. Original Trace sections exist today thanks to its curious composition—in some places its narrow clay bed has been cut down to a depth of thirty feet.

Of the writers living along this most romantic and historic of American highways, perhaps none has written so imaginatively of it as Eudora Welty, whose native Jackson, Miss., lies on the Trace. Among the newest of American writers and author of several promising volumes of short stories, she excels (in the words of Katherine Anne Porter, to whom she has been compared) "in showing where an external act and the internal voiceless life of the human imagination almost meet and mingle on the mysterious threshold between dream and waking." Into many of her stories Eudora Welty has woven the dreamlike Natchez Trace, in whose shadowy, leafy hollows she played not too long ago.

A writer who developed quietly, apart from any "school," Eudora Welty is nevertheless a member of that group—the Southern writers—currently dominating the American literary scene.

Steep clay banks flank the Old Natchez Trace, once main route to the Mississippi and the Southwest.

They walked through the still leaves of the Natchez Trace, the light and the shade falling through trees about them, the white irises shining like candles on the banks and the new ferns shining like green stars up in the oak branches . . .

—LIVVIE

ACKNOWLEDGMENTS

Grateful acknowledgment is made to the many people who assisted in the preparation of this book from its earliest stages to its completion, the hospitable souls throughout America, too numerous to mention but not forgotten, who gave us a night's lodging or pointed out a route or possible picture. Our thanks are due the Editors of *Life* for permission to use the Willa Cather material on pages 120 to 122, and to Hilde Adeslberger and Charles Tudor of that publication for their helpful advice on layout and typography. Our thanks go also to the staff of the New York Public Library for months of assistance in research and writing. We are particularly grateful to Prof. Kenneth Robinson of the Dartmouth College English Department for his suggestions in the initial choice of subject matter and his final reading of the galleys although final responsibility for statements or opinions rests with the authors. The following publishers are acknowledged, with deep thanks, for permission to include quotations from their authors' works:

Excerpt from "The Old Swimmin' Hole" by James Whitcomb Riley from *Neighborly Poems,* reprinted by courtesy of The Bobbs-Merrill Company, Inc.; excerpts from *The Cop and the Anthem* by O. Henry and *McTeague* by Frank Norris reprinted by courtesy of Doubleday & Company, Inc.; excerpts from *Riders of the Purple Sage* by Zane Grey, *The Rise of Silas Lapham* by William Dean Howells, *The American Scene* by Henry James, *Washington Square* by Henry James, *Giants in the Earth* by Ole Rölvaag, and *Native Son* by Richard Wright reprinted by courtesy of Harper & Brothers; excerpts from *The Education of Henry Adams, O Pioneers* by Willa Cather, and *The Tory Lover* by Sarah Orne Jewett used by permission of the publishers, Houghton Mifflin Company; excerpt from "Burying Ground by the Ties" from Archibald MacLeish's *Poems 1924–1933* used by permission of the publishers, Houghton Mifflin Company; excerpt from *The Iron Heel* by Jack London reprinted by courtesy of the Jack London Ranch; excerpts from "Smoke" from *Knight's Gambit* by William Faulkner, *Absalom, Absalom!* by William Faulkner, *A Rose for Emily* by William Faulkner, *The Unvanquished* by William Faulkner, *Tor House* by Robinson Jeffers, and *Melanctha* by Gertrude Stein reprinted by courtesy of Random House, Inc.; excerpts from *The Hoosier Schoolmaster* by Edward Eggleston, *The End of Something* by Ernest Hemingway, *To Have and Have Not* by Ernest Hemingway, *The Last Tycoon* by F. Scott Fitzgerald, *The Golden Honeymoon* by Ring Lardner, *Gullible's Travels* by Ring Lardner, *The Yearling* by Marjorie Kinnan Rawlings, *Ethan Frome* by Edith Wharton, and *Look Homeward, Angel* by Thomas Wolfe reprinted by courtesy of Charles Scribner's Sons; excerpts from *Winesburg, Ohio* by Sherwood Anderson, *The Jungle* by Upton Sinclair, and *The Grapes of Wrath* by John Steinbeck reprinted by courtesy of The Viking Press.

THE ASBESTOS & MAGNESIA